Cold Mountain

The Journey from Book to Film

Men ask the way to Cold Mountain.
Cold Mountain: there's no through trail.
                                        —HAN-SHAN

Cold Mountain

The Journey from Book to Film

FOREWORD BY CHARLES FRAZIER

INTRODUCTION BY ANTHONY MINGHELLA

PHOTOGRAPHS BY PHIL BRAY, DEMMIE TODD AND BRIGITTE LACOMBE

EDITED BY LINDA SUNSHINE   DESIGNED BY TIMOTHY SHANER

CONTRIBUTING WRITERS DAN AUILER AND LARRY KAPLAN

A NEWMARKET PICTORIAL MOVIEBOOK

NEWMARKET PRESS
NEW YORK

This book is published in the United States of America.

First Edition

10 9 8 7 6 5 4 3 2 1

ISBN: 1-55704-593-3

Library of Congress Cataloging-in-Publication Data available upon request.

QUANTITY PURCHASES

Companies, professional groups, clubs, and other organizations may qualify
for special terms when ordering quantities of this title. For information,
write Special Sales Department, Newmarket Press, 18 East 48th Street,
New York, NY 10017; call (212) 832-3575; fax (212) 832-3629;
or e-mail mailbox@newmarketpress.com.

www.newmarketpress.com

Design by Timothy Shaner.

Manufactured in the United States of America.

Other Newmarket Pictorial Moviebooks include:

Hulk: The illustrated Screenplay

The Art of X2

Gods and Generals: The Illustrated Story of the Epic Civil War Film

Chicago: The Movie and Lyrics

Catch Me If You Can: The Film and the Filmmakers

Frida: Bringing Frida Kahlo's Life and Art to Film

*E.T. The Extra-Terrestrial from Concept to Classic:
The Illustrated Story of the Film and the Filmmakers*

*Windtalkers: The Making of the Film about the
Navajo Code Talkers of World War II*

Ali: The Movie and the Man

Planet of the Apes: Re-imagined by Tim Burton

*Moulin Rouge: The Splendid Book That Charts
the Journey of Baz Luhrmann's Motion Picture*

The Art of The Matrix

Gladiator: The Making of the Ridley Scott Epic

Crouching Tiger, Hidden Dragon: A Portrait of the Ang Lee Film

*Titus: The Illustrated Screenplay, Adapted
from the Play by William Shakespeare*

*The Age of Innocence: A Portrait of the Film
Based on the Novel by Edith Wharton*

Cradle Will Rock: The Movie and the Moment

Saving Private Ryan: The Men, the Mission, the Movie

Amistad: A Celebration of the Film by Steven Spielberg

Bram Stoker's Dracula: The Film and the Legend

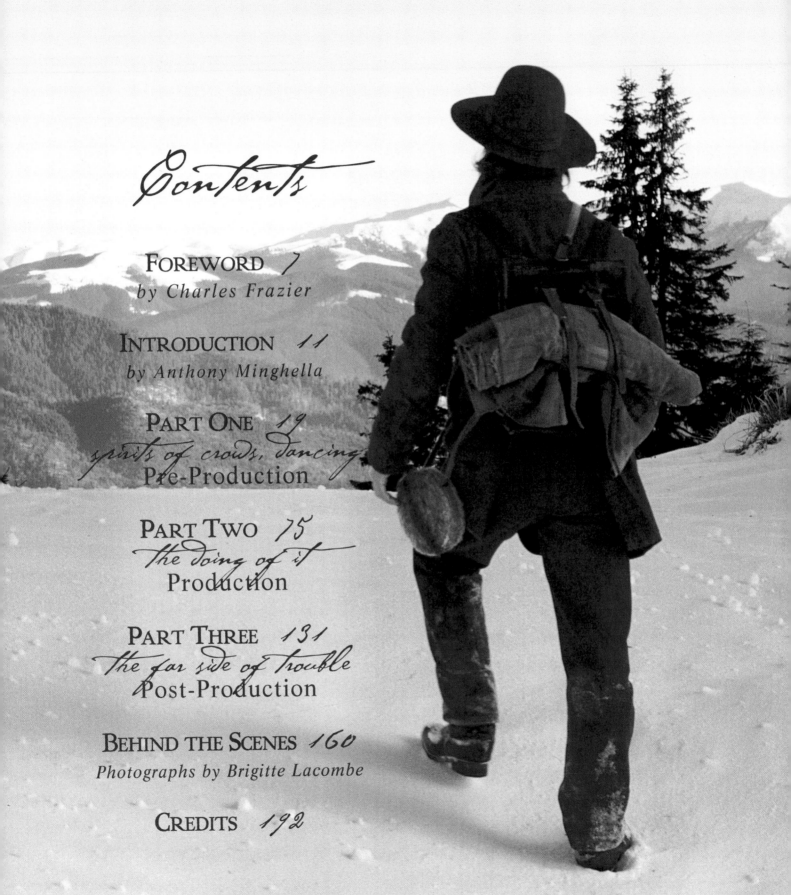

Contents

Foreword

by Charles Frazier

Writing is a solitary business. At its most basic level, a novel is one person sitting alone in a room many hours a day for several years. My daughter's most vivid memories of the time of our lives when I was working on *Cold Mountain* are the countless winter evenings she came home from school after sunset. The house would be dark but for one light in the window of my office.

On the other hand, any movie of considerable physical scope is the work of hundreds, perhaps thousands, of people. I saw just a fraction of the filming of this movie, a few days out of the nearly six months during which the cameras were rolling, but my strongest impression was of the unimaginable amount of human effort being expended in the effort to get things right. The moment this struck me most clearly was one November day in Romania when Dante Ferretti, production designer for the movie, took me to see the town he designed and built—several dozen structures far off in a remote mountain valley.

Filming at that location ended weeks before my visit, and I'm told that wolves have been seen on the main street. It is snowing when we arrive. Just a car-load of us wander the empty town. The buildings are not façades, but are com-pletely and meticulously furnished. We walk into the store, and inside is the complete cluttered stock of a nineteenth-century mercantile. We go to the boarding house and into Inman's room where there are still linens on the bed. I imagine this valley filled with workers building this town, then becoming even more crowded with cast, crew, and extras during filming, an extensive base-camp of tents and trailers down the hill supplying the needs of the movie and of its several hundred people, a temporary village created for a brief period by this job.

The snow is falling harder, beginning to cover the dirt street. On a hill above the town is a replica of a nineteenth-century church that stands in western North Carolina. I went there with Dante several autumns ago. He photographed and measured it inside and out, pulled the rope and rang the bell in the steeple. When we walk into the reconstruction I say, "Dante, this is exactly the same." He says, "No. It's six feet longer. To allow room for the cameras."

In a novel it is possible to suggest a location with just a few brush strokes—three or four vivid, carefully chosen details, and the reader imagines the rest. The camera, though, is bru-

tally literal. It cannot suggest what is not there. It demands a fully realized world confronting it frame by frame. This elaborate Romanian ghost town, the work of so many, will be on screen for perhaps ten minutes. Now it is a husk the camera has left behind.

This all seems a long time and a long way from January 1998 when Anthony Minghella and I stood in light rain trying to hitch a ride after a hike in a somewhat remote corner of the North Carolina mountains. As I recall, we had been talking about movies in general rather than this movie, which was still quite hypothetical at the time. A man out fishing gave us a lift back to my car in his pick-up. He was a shy old mountaineer, and when we got out he was awkward with our thank-you handshakes, as if he found eye contact and the touch of skin to skin too familiar for comfort. My gas tank was nearly empty, with many miles of dirt between it and the nearest station. But the CD player was filled with old-time Appalachian music—Tommy Jarrell, Tim O'Brien, and Dirk Powell—so things balanced out.

Back then, it never occurred to me that a movie adaptation of my novel would be filmed anywhere outside the Southern Appalachians. In hindsight, that was naïve. The realities and the economies of filmmaking are what they are. I was told that the Carpathians looked strikingly like western North Carolina, only more primitive. So I went.

And I found that there are places in Romania where you feel momentarily thrown back into an old agricultural world most of us have forgotten, a time prior to electricity and the internal combustion engine and maybe even steam power. And then the next minute, on a narrow mountain road, a brand new BMW 745 blows past a horse cart hauling firewood. You'll pass

—Then tell me of

a big-box Wal-Mart–style store, the parking lot full of Dacias and Toyotas, people hustling in to buy stuff, talking on cell phones. Same as home. And then within five miles, shepherds in huge medieval dread-locked sheepskin coats and long crooked staffs drive their flocks down the fields. Cattle wander the dark streets of unlighted towns without supervision on the way to their stalls. At the hotel, the desk clerk, who speaks three languages and seems to work around the clock, is paid sixty dollars a month. Everywhere you go, heartbreaking stray dogs forage for food. Nearly every radio station plays techno-disco. All the Romanians I talk with for any length of time eventually speak about leaving. But if you hold your head just right and see only what the camera sees, now and then bits of the place do bear some resemblance to western North Carolina.

As I write this, I have not seen the finished movie; but after all, this book is about the process, not the product. I would simply like to conclude by acknowledging all of the people in the cast and crew who worked for so long, mostly outdoors in very difficult physical conditions—the hundred degree heat of July and the zero degree cold of December. Many of them I met, perhaps on a steamy day in Charleston or huddled around a kerosene heater in Romania, the ground a mess of mud and cables. Many showed me battle-scarred copies of my book—dog-eared, water-wrinkled. They all have my thanks for their art and craft and hard work.

your long journey home, Ada said.

Introduction

by Anthony Minghella

Six years ago, while spending an idyllic few days reading, swimming, and musing with my friend Michael Ondaatje at his cabin near Toronto, Michael handed me a proof copy of Charles Frazier's *Cold Mountain* with a recommendation from its publisher. Destined for a modest hardback release, the manuscript—the work of a first-time novelist—had attracted no serious film interest (the same had been true of *The English Patient*). When I returned to London another copy of the book was waiting for me, this time sent by Sydney Pollack and Bill Horberg at Mirage. I took this as an omen. I read the book. The prose is like denim, made for work; serious steadfast sentences that talk of the land, of loss, of a terrible damage to the country, the end of something. There's a resolute man walking home to find the woman who waits has also changed, irrevocably, in his absence. It is a story that makes you want to go walking.

Nature is brought into the reader's room by *Cold Mountain* with visceral power. I can't ever remember having been made to feel so alert to changes in temperature, altitude, or the seasons. Flakes of snow fall in the pages with tragic consequences. It announces itself as a masculine book, reverent about the workings of guns and tools, about the way to skin a hog, hunt a bear, read a trail. But it is the women who stay in the mind, Ada and Ruby, remarkable and original creations, flinty, clear, and funny. I was mesmerized. A week later a sudden rally of interest led to an auction in which the price for the film rights escalated. In a telephone conversation I spoke to Charles Frazier about my passionate regard for the novel and my profound ignorance of the period or the landscape in which it was set. I knew nothing either about the causes or effects of the American Civil War. This seemed to amuse him and the next day United Artists acquired the rights for me with Mirage and Ron Yerxa and Albert Berger's Bona Fide to produce. By that Christmas there were a million and a half copies of *Cold Mountain* in print, it stood at the top of the *The New York Times* best seller list, had won the National Book Award, and was a publishing phenomenon. *Cold Mountain* fever had gripped America.

Frazier's genius had been to cast his account of a deserting Confederate soldier's journey home in the shape of *The Odyssey*, or rather to see in the true story of his ancestor's walk through the state of North Carolina at the end of the Civil War resonant parallels with Homer's epic poem. The book has the quality of myth, as if it has always been there, as if the book itself had been discovered on the trail to Cold Mountain (a

LEFT: Anthony Minghella and Nicole Kidman on location in Romania.
ABOVE: Minghella and Jude Law.

real place, incidentally, and once partly owned by Frazier's great great uncle, W. P. Inman, who gives the protagonist his name). It is by turns unflinchingly violent and intensely tender. A very cruel book. I took advice before I committed to taking it on. One friend recounted how, after reading it, she had wailed so much in the night that her children had come into her bedroom to see why she was crying; another was so incensed by the events of the last pages that he threw the book across the room. This seemed promising.

Boiled down to its armature, the book makes an irresistible case for adaptation to the screen: an honourable man, a journey, a purpose, a series of obstacles, someone waiting with forbearance, and Cold Mountain itself, a place which becomes more than a place, becomes a goal, stands in for a time and way of life which have been lost. At its heart the book has a question: Is it better to have tried and failed than never to have tried at all? A blind man finds Inman's notion of a few minutes' gift of sight to be an appalling one. Undaunted, Inman sets off, deserting the Rebels and a pointless, hopeless war, to get sight of Cold Mountain. In a lawless world—the violence stunningly casual, nature indifferent—only an indomitable cussedness pushes Inman forward. In its effortless flexing between epic sweep and the minute details of

the landscape, in its insistence on the relation between the private world and the public one, *Cold Mountain* goes a long way toward earning the instant classic status it has attained in America.

I went to North Carolina and visited Frazier. During the course of an inspiring week I discovered a man as careful with the words he speaks as he is with the ones he commits to paper. He has walked Inman's paths and showed me some of them. Looking out at Grandfather Mountain, the most distinctive of the Blue Ridge peaks in western North Carolina, we discussed the movie. At this point I was in architect mode. I had made a breakdown of the key scenes and sequences in the novel, but if each one was allocated only five minutes of screen time, the film was already four hours long. There would have to be amputations. And the chronology would have to be simplified. Some characters would have to go, some amalgamated, some have their functions altered. I had to work on the book with a tape measure, a compass, and a scalpel. Sitting with Charles Frazier on the porch where most of his novel was written, the mountains in front of us shrouded in mist, I was conscious of a strange moment, as if I were adopting someone's child. I was starting the long and painful journey to turn Charles Frazier's *Cold Mountain* into something of my own.

ABOVE: Partners Sydney Pollack and Anthony Minghella on location in Romania.

Adaptation is an act of thievery. Beautiful stories are plundered, seemingly in the most perverse ways. The literature, a novel's flesh, the very thing that makes the novel memorable, is discarded. The screenwriter is more concerned with the gristle of situation, with the small bones of the story's architecture. To this end, I have developed a dubious, but superstitiously held technique in which I force myself to write without the book at hand, so determined am I not to be captivated by the prose, or its contours. The filmmaker must approach the job as a storyteller with an exciting new tale meeting an audience anxious to be caught up in the way of telling, its rhythms and dynamics; to be transported to a special world, immediate, urgent, and with authority. The novel's delicious peregrinations, its asides, its tricks with point of view, must remain within its pages. And the film can proceed with the special confidence that the best screen adaptations lead the audience inexorably back to the source material, that the book remains unscathed, waiting to be discovered and appreciated. Viewers of *Cold Mountain* can become readers of Charles Frazier's book.

Film, meanwhile, must assert its own vocabulary, notably its ability to create ellipsis, where a film sentence, a specific series of shots and perspectives are joined together in sequences from which an audience infers narrative and meaning. The gaps, the information withheld, are where the audience participates in meaning, and the elegance of these ellipses often determines the degree of pleasure experienced by the viewer. These economies, deftly used, can be thrilling. They can accelerate narrative at a rate that would leave a reader breathless. And the audience, more sophisticated at decoding moving image than in any other medium, continues to need fewer and fewer clues before it is willing and able to extrapolate meaning. Looking at movies from forty years ago it is almost touching to examine film grammar and see how much more information was deemed necessary to establish transparent narrative. Actors walk through doors, are seen to sit down; a scene occurs; the actors get up and are seen to leave the room. All the narrative action is collected. Today simply the impulse to leave is enough to prompt a cut and we glue together the proceeding shot (a car roars off, for example) as a continuous action. We have learned to interpret a multitude of disjointed disparate events as something coherent.

The making of any film is the story of folly prevailing over common sense. Films take too long to make and cost too much. They are frail dreams remorselessly complicated by the contingent demands of practicality. The makers of films are hostage to the intractability of those who must sell them, and vice-versa. Art lies down with commerce, both furtively planning betrayals. The sanctuary of the editing room, where decisions are mostly pure and sometimes pious, gives way to the bordello of the preview screening, where directors would happily surrender their most fiercely held ideal for a favourable reception.

It is always possible as a director to feel the hubris and loneliness of authorship.

Nevertheless, a glance at the interminable list of credits at the end of even the most modest movie serves as a bracing reminder of the number of people who have been enlisted to create an event sometimes attributed to one artist's vision. This book further illuminates the confluence of efforts, the stamina, and the devotion required to bring a movie into the cinema. It really is a labour of love for those behind and in front of the camera. And the salutary part is that all this remarkable effort is never any guarantee of success.

Creating a period film carries with it daunting imperatives—the painstaking re-creation of time and place and the attendant dangers of autopsy that accompany the process. In the very way that the contemporary movie is almost always careless of its period, with the confidence that nothing glimpsed in the frame can be wrong, so the period film is often guilty of zealous and reverent observation, informed by the imperative that everything in the frame must sing of period. This can lead to the museum-like characteristics of so many films set in the past, where metonymic shots dominate—each sequence straining to find some opportunity to illus-

trate history. Rigorously avoiding this pitfall informed many of the decisions of the production team on *Cold Mountain*, forcing them as it did to create throwaway environments, glanced at, sometimes ignored, so that the audience can feel the period and not be assaulted by it.

The result of work is, of course, the point of all this effort but, finally, it is abstract, experienced by others. For the filmmakers it is the process that makes up a life, which defines the film. The doing lasts four or five years; the result a matter of hours. And it is that process, and the celebration of the incredible team with whom I am lucky enough to work, that makes for the most intriguing part of what follows. The unity of purpose described in these pages comes first from an almost unqualified regard for Charles Frazier's novel and then from the mysteries of individual ownership of the same project. The film is claimed, repeatedly, by different people. The producers assemble a team, the screenwriter writes, the designer creates a world, the costume designer creates its inhabitants, the director directs, the actors move and speak, the cinematographer photographs, the sound recordist captures sounds, the editor selects and weaves together the mosaic of images, the composer responds and accompanies. And so on. Along the way, each worker is required to contribute fully, from the animal handlers to the

ABOVE: Nicole Kidman and Anthony Minghella on location in Romania. RIGHT: Minghella oversees production on location.

Introduction

special effects team and for each department there is a prevailing sense that their contribution is vital. And it is. For the film's greensman this was a story about crop rotation, the cycle of the seasons. For the property master it was a film about tintype photographs and fiddler crabs. It is as if the movie is its own book and that each sentence relies on a letter carefully fashioned by a separate team, often in a different place and at a different time.

I am writing this at the music recording studio at Abbey Road in London where, in an otherwise empty studio, a sole percussionist is painstakingly adding a timpani roll to Gabriel Yared's overture for the film's credit sequence. It is a particularly appropriate accompaniment to a preface about how movies are made. A much-repeated anecdote concerns an interview in which a director was asked what he considered to be the most important ingredient of a successful movie. His emphatic reply was that 50 percent of the job was getting the right screenplay and 50 percent casting the right actors. The journalist nodded. And 50 percent the right locations, continued the director, and 50 percent the right score. And 50 percent the right cinematographer, etc. Today, in the closing gestures of postproduction on *Cold Mountain*, it is about where the inflection on the timpani should come for this fleeting moment early in the movie, and seven people doing different jobs sit in the booth, listening, wrangling, contemplating the image on the monitors above us. Elsewhere in London, editor Walter Murch is cutting in some visual effects, cinematographer John Seale is working on the grading of the images, ADR supervisor Mark Levinson is preparing cues for the last remaining actors to re-

record pieces of their dialogue, the sound department is preparing tracks for the final mix. In New York, the marketing department works on the trailer and promotional material. In Los Angeles, designer Deb Ross is creating titles. The army continues its march. This fascinating book, already a document of nostalgia for me with its evocations of Romania and the American South, with its contributions from the key creative team, elaborates any insights I might have and is poignant in reminding me of how much of the movie is created away from my own invasive supervision. Most of all it goes some way toward disinterring the complex equation of movie-making and celebrating what is, for me, the most rewarding element of a bruising but beautiful adventure: the joy of collaboration, the buoyant camaraderie that has held my spirits even when they were battered by the weather gods, by the limitations of my own talent and by the absurd ambition of creating a piece of art that must also return to the studio the huge sum of money invested in *Cold Mountain*. This book is the souvenir of that attempt, in photographs, but also in the words of the film family who have climbed a mountain together. And leading us throughout, most exposed, have been the actors. When we have all disappeared, their faces will remain. And it is in Jude, Nicole, Renée, and all their colleagues in our marvelous cast that the true and intrepid spirit of the journey is captured.

LEFT: Scene from the beginning of the movie when Jude Law first sees Nicole Kidman. ABOVE: Tintype of Jude Law by Stephen Berkman that was used as a prop in the movie.

spirits of crows, dancing

PART ONE

Pre-Production

pacing, patience, rhythm

Ada had wondered if they had strength for such work, but Ruby argued in detail that it did not necessarily require pure power. Just pacing, patience, rhythm. Pull the saw and release. Wait for the one at the other end of the saw to draw it away and then pull again. Avoid binding up. The main thing, Ruby said, was not to get ahead of yourself. Go at a rhythm that could be sustained on and on. Do just as much as you could do and still be able to get up and again tomorrow. No more, and no less.

—CHARLES FRAZIER, FROM HIS NOVEL

source and root

From Novel to Screenplay

Charles Frazier's first novel, *Cold Mountain*, was published in 1997 by Grove Press. A complex and enthralling adventure, the book is also a stirring love story and a luminous evocation of a vanished American landscape.

Cold Mountain describes the relentless journey of a young Confederate soldier named Inman who, after four torturous years of battle bravely fought, is severely wounded and disillusioned. He decides to abandon the Civil War and walk hundreds of miles to return to his home in Cold Mountain. "Inman's journey is toward a vision he has of peace, home, and a way of life," says Charles Frazier. Along the way, Inman's faith, strength, and courage are continually tested as he encounters an astonishing array of characters.

Simultaneously, the novel tells of another pilgrimage, the journey of Ada, the woman waiting at home for Inman. Her journey is measured in millimeters when compared to the length of Inman's trip but it is equally profound. At the start of the story Ada is a person of privilege. Cultured and refined, she can speak foreign languages, play the piano, and paint with watercolors but she can't wash her clothes or cook a meal. "I can embroider but I can't darn, I can arrange cut flowers but I can't grow them," Ada says in Anthony Minghella's screenplay. "If a thing has a function, if I might do something with it, it wasn't considered suitable." In the course of the story, Ada must transform herself, she must learn how to survive a heartless war and become wise in the ways of nature. Ada's journey is guided by an equally diverse group of characters, especially Ruby, a near feral mountain woman of rare fortitude and grace.

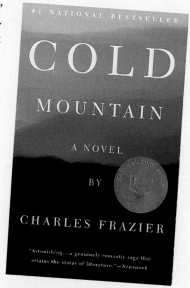

Powerful and compelling, the novel was hailed upon publication as a literary masterpiece by critics such as Alfred Kazin. "Frazier's feeling for the Southern landscape is reverential and beautifully composed," Kazin wrote in *The New York Review of Books*. "He has written an astonishing first novel."

The New York Times Book Review called *Cold Mountain* "a Whitmanesque foray into America: into its hugeness, its freshness, its scope and its soul." *The Raleigh News & Observer* considered it "as close to a masterpiece as American writing is going to come these days."

Soon enough the novel appeared on *The New York Times* bestseller list. Then, in November 1997, *Cold Mountain* was awarded the National Book Award for fiction and went on to become one of the most popular books of the year.

Although this scenario is probably every author's dream come true, the success of this first novel, written by a virtually unknown Southern academic, was understandably overwhelming

LEFT: Renée Zellweger and Nicole Kidman on location in Rasnov, Romania, where the Black Cove farm was constructed. ABOVE: The paperback edition of Charles Frazier's award-winning novel.

for the writer himself. "It was a heady experience for an author who had spent so much time alone working on the novel," Frazier explains. "Then, to be suddenly thrust into this world of book signings, readings, and interest from film studios; it was almost more than I could comprehend at the time."

In the end, *Cold Mountain* spent more than a year and a half on the *The New York Times* bestseller list, turning into something of a publishing phenomenon and attracting readers all over the world. Today it is routinely taught in high schools and universities all across the country.

There is nothing more precious to filmmakers than an enthralling story filled with complex characters so it was no surprise that *Cold Mountain* attracted the attention of Hollywood long before it was a literary or financial phenomena. Successful film producers like Albert Berger are constantly on the lookout for such properties. One day in 1997 Berger discovered Frazier's book while he was browsing the bookshelves in the Sunset Strip's Book Soup store.

"Glancing at the inner flap I found it very interesting because it's about a part of the country where I spent a lot of time, the Blue Ridge Mountains and the Appalachians of North Carolina," Berger says. "I'm also interested in the Civil War. So I bought the book and read it. I knew immediately I wanted to make it into a film."

Berger showed *Cold Mountain* to his Bona Fide Films partner, Ron Yerxa, with whom he had produced *Election* in 1999. Yerxa shared Berger's enthusiasm, and after making a few

calls, they discovered that Frazier's manuscript had already been sent to various Hollywood studios, all of which had passed on it. In fact, Charles Frazier had declined an offer from an independent film company, so the rights were still available. With glowing initial reviews, the book showed steadily growing sales and was on the verge of hitting the bestseller lists. For the producers, time was of the essence.

"*Cold Mountain* works on a large canvas and tells an epic story, so Ron and I saw this as a studio movie, not as a small independent effort," Berger says. The two producers immediately submitted *Cold Mountain* to William Horberg, a producer at Sydney Pollack's Mirage Enterprises, hoping that Pollack would be interested in directing the project. Pollack was in London at the time shooting Stanley Kubrick's *Eyes Wide Shut*. "I received the book on a Monday and was asked to read it right away," says Pollack, "but there was really no way I was going to have time to read the book before we needed to move on it, so Bill and I decided to send the book to Anthony." Mirage was developing *The Talented Mr. Ripley* with the English

ABOVE: Producers Sydney Pollack and Bill Horberg on location in Romania.

writer and director Anthony Minghella, and looking to extend their relationship with him.

In a bit of serendipity, Minghella had received a copy of *Cold Mountain* that very weekend from his friend, Michael Ondaatje, the author of *The English Patient*.

"Michael and I had been traveling together, having a weekend of reading plays and poetry, when he told me, 'My publisher says you should read this book. You'll like it very much,'" Minghella explains. "The next thing I know, Bill and Sydney called to tell me that Albert and Ron sent them the same book and they really wanted me to read it. Then, when I returned home to London, yet another copy was waiting for me that had been sent by United Artists. So within a week I received three copies of the same book. I thought that must mean something and that I had better read it."

Even with such prophetic coincidences, Minghella confesses that, at first, he was reluctant to consider the project. "It was at a time when, after making *The English Patient* and getting ready to shoot the script I wrote for *The Talented Mr. Ripley*, I had decided that I wouldn't do any more adaptations," explains the director. "I thought I should go back to my own work."

Despite his reluctance to take on yet another adaptation, Minghella was intrigued by Frazier's book. "I realized at once that it was a great novel, unique and extraordinary, and it spoke to me about preoccupations that were prominent in my mind at the time," he explains. "I had been doing some writing about the idea of pilgrimage. Also, at the time I had been reading a wonderful Canadian poet, Anne Carson, who had written a long narrative work about the pilgrimage of St. James. The concept of pilgrimage fascinated me. I had been a teacher of medieval theater history at university and was familiar with a great deal of the dramatized Christian fiction of the time that was connected with viewing man on a journey.

"The most famous play of that period is called *Every Man*, but there are many versions of this metaphor that Man is on the road of life; to the left of him are the possibilities of virtue and, to the right, are the possibilities of vice. The decision to stay on the road or to stray off course becomes, then, a kind of paradigm of existence.

"Another thing that struck me profoundly was the Chinese epigraph at the opening the book," Minghella continues. "'Men ask the way to Cold Mountain. Cold Mountain: there's no easy route.' My wife is Chinese and I'm intrigued by Chinese literature. She told me that in Buddhist poetry Cold Mountain is a spiritual destination. It's nirvana."

The more he read, the more Minghella understood that the book's themes were both multifaceted and, even more critical, eminently cinematic.

ABOVE: Clockwise from left: Associate producer Timothy Bricknell, producer Ron Yerxa, Jude Law, Anthony Minghella, script supervisor Dianne Dreyer.

To some extent, I always thought of *Cold Mountain*
as a meditation on what we fear and desire, the way we
react to violence on a personal level and how we move
away from violence towards peace, home, and a way
of life. I think those are not particularly time-bound
concerns. The Civil War gave me a concrete background,
but any violent conflict could offer similar stories.

—CHARLES FRAZIER

"One thing that intrigued me about reading the book was that the story, at first, seems to be about one thing but then it quickly becomes apparent that it's about something else," Minghella says. "It appears to be a story about the American Civil War. In truth, I don't necessarily have an interest in war stories but then I realized that war was not the central issue at all.

"*Cold Mountain* is about a man returning from war, so the story is really about the aftermath of war and the effect of war on the world away from the battlefield. I realized I was in territory that is very, very interesting—and very fresh.

"The journey of Inman [whose name is not unlike Everyman] is also one of a series of tests—he's tested by hubris, by courage, by vanity, by romantic love, by his coarse desires and by his loyalty. Inman is on a spiritual journey and I realized the book was an American version of *The Odyssey* in so far as it's about a man who's weary of war, who's been away from home longer than he ever expected. Inman struggles to return home but every conceivable obstacle is placed in front of him."

Minghella also found a personal connection in the character of Ada. "As much as I identify with Inman—or as much as I project onto Inman what it would be like to be a warrior returning home—I also identify with Ada. I feel as if I have an extremely nourished inner life and an undernourished outer life. I'm relatively ignorant about working the land or working with animals so I could relate to Ada's situation and the challenges she must face.

"As a director, I always gravitate toward film projects where I feel the material is beyond me at first glance. With *Cold Mountain*, I was offered an enormous opportunity, as a filmmaker living in England, to make a movie about the most critical and defining event of American history: the Civil War. Here I could also explore my own relationship to nature. One of the most appealing aspects of taking on *Cold Mountain* was the opportunity to educate myself not only about American history but also about the rigors of the physical world."

By now convinced that he wanted to film Frazier's book, Minghella needed to commit to the project right away. Several other major filmmakers were also eager to bring *Cold Mountain* to the screen, and competing offers were being made for the property. Though the competition was fierce, author Charles Frazier had been very impressed with Anthony Minghella.

"I knew from Michael Ondaatje what a wonderful experience he had had with Anthony on *The English Patient*," Frazier says. "When I met Anthony in London I thought it would be a

ABOVE: Jude Law and producer Albert Berger. RIGHT: Nicole Kidman and Donald Sutherland in one of the opening scenes of the movie.

perfect match because Anthony came to movies by way of books. I felt he would be able to make the material his own, which has to happen for a movie to succeed. At the same time, though, I knew Anthony respected what I had written."

When the Mirage/Bona Fide team, with Minghella writing and directing and UA financing, was presented to Frazier, he chose this group to make the movie from his novel. The deal was signed in July of 1997.

"I was thrilled that Anthony decided to do it," Sydney Pollack says. "*Cold Mountain* is a story I would've been interested in directing myself because it's the kind of film that both Anthony and I treasure. It's a love story at heart, but it's also an adventure story about a torturous journey, an odyssey that tests a man in every way possible. But at its center, it's an examination of the inhumanity of war. That's a great combination and a hard one to find."

Despite everyone's enthusiasm about the deal that was finalized in the summer of 1997, progress on the film was stalled for a time because of Minghella's previous commitments. First, he had to shoot and then oversee post-production on *The Talented Mr. Ripley* (which was released in 1999). Also, he, Pollack, and Horberg were busy producing several films at Mirage. It wasn't until late into 2000 that the writer/director had time to work exclusively on his *Cold Mountain* screenplay. He completed a first draft in March of 2001.

Pollack was among the first to read the screenplay and was among the first to appreciate the rare talents Minghella brings to his work. "Anthony is able to make his adaptation completely his own without ever violating the author's intent," Pollack says. "In a way, Anthony re-imagines and re-dreams the whole world of the novel."

According to producer Bill Horberg, Minghella's process in creating a screenplay is to remember the pleasure he experienced reading the book and then find a way to communicate that feeling to the readers of his screenplay and, ultimately, to the audience of the movie. "Having worked with Anthony on *The Talented Mr. Ripley* I came to know his unusual gifts as an adapter of novels," says Horberg. "He reads a novel deeply, several times, but then he puts it aside and sits down to write without referring to it at all. Minghella wants to capture the intentions of the author, and the spirit and theme of the book but having put the book aside as he writes, he liberates himself and creates on his own terms without once referring back to the novel."

One of the screenwriter's greatest challenges in adapting the novel was the sequencing of the story line. "The way I tell the story is not the way Charles tells the story," Minghella explains. "I was concerned with sketching out the film's central theme—returning soldier and

ABOVE: Minghella and John Seale, director of photography.

28

Filmmaking plays into a personality type. I enjoy being alone and I get to spend great deal of time alone, when I am writing. In fact, I get sort of agoraphobic. But I also love working collectively. The rhythm of being a writer and director requires that I spend half the time by myself—writing and editing—and then a period of enormous social activity. My personality was designed for this job. Good or not, what it offers me is a very good fit.

—ANTHONY MINGHELLA

waiting woman." Minghella's problem was complicated. When the story begins, Ada and Inman have been separated for four years. Yet the story required that the filmmaker define this central relationship before it was severed by the war. "The screenplay struggled with trying to establish this relationship without overwhelming the story," admits Minghella.

Minghella's solution was to tell the story out of sequence, through a complex narrative that allows the relationship that develops between Ada and Inman to be intercut with Inman's involvement in the Civil War. This structure allowed for the film's back story—Ada and Inman falling in love, Inman getting wounded and the death of Ada's father—to be woven together in the first section of the film so that once Inman begins his journey home, the film moves forward in a straight narrative.

Clearly, he had solved the problem. The first draft of Minghella's completed screenplay was considered a major accomplishment by everyone involved in the project. "Reading a Minghella screenplay is totally unique and unlike reading any other screenwriter," says Horberg. "His own preoccupations and concerns find their way into the text in a kind of wonderful marriage of the narrative of the novel and the director's own sensibility. He's a deeply humanistic writer, concerned with the real emotions of his characters, and with re-creating their complex psychology. There are no white or black hats in his movies. Minghella's people are multi-dimensional."

Perhaps the most demanding critic, or at least the person with the most vested interest in the story, the author of the novel, also supported the screenplay. "Charles Frazier read the script and expressed a lot of contentment," says Sydney Pollack, "and everyone else who read it felt the same." The script was approved in May of 2001.

By now, UA was no longer involved in the production of the picture. MGM had taken over the picture from UA. Then, under new management, MGM decided to partner with Miramax on the production. Miramax had backed both *The English Patient* and *The Talented Mr. Ripley* (in partnership with Paramount Pictures). Unable to come to terms with Miramax on the budget, MGM dropped out as a partner around commencement of principal photography in the

summer of 2002. And Miramax took over the project. When Miramax chairman Harvey Weinstein read Minghella's screenplay he was unstinting in his praise.

With the screenplay completed and the studio in place, the project was ready to move forward. The next twelve months, from May of 2001 to May of 2002, would be used to prepare for production, set to begin in the summer of 2002 and continue through December. Progress began on several fronts simultaneously. June and July of 2001 were spent assembling a working crew by arranging for Minghella to reunite with his Academy Award-winning production team from *The English Patient*: editor Walter Murch, direc-

tor of photography John Seale, costume designer Ann Roth, composer Gabriel Yared, first assistant director and associate producer Steve Andrews, and script supervisor, Dianne Dreyer. All of these multi-talented people had also worked together on *The Talented Mr. Ripley*. They were joined on *Cold Mountain* by five-time Academy Award-nominated production designer Dante Ferretti and Iain Smith, the executive line producer, who would play a critical role in figuring out how to make a large historical epic within the movie's budget restraints.

Anthony Minghella is the first to admit that assembling a core production team of the best professionals is the key component to his success as a filmmaker. "One of the best qualities I have as a director is that I think I've been quite shrewd in surrounding myself with very talented people on my films who can teach me things, who are experienced and who know their departments in a way I never could," Minghella explains. "I felt very lucky to be able to have them on board for this film. These people are essential for me. This is my kitchen cabinet of collaborators; they are very demanding and expect a lot of me."

With his collaborators in place, Minghella faced two more extremely challenging tasks before filming could get underway—casting the film and selecting the locations.

"The two things I dread most as I get near filming are casting and scouting," Minghella confesses. "The dread comes simply from the amount of energy I know is going to be expended to accomplish these tasks. Casting is heartbreaking because of the number of actors we have to reject, and scouting is difficult because of the number of miles we have to travel and the number of locations we ultimately turn down."

And so, the hardest part of Minghella's journey to bring *Cold Mountain* to the screen was about to begin in earnest.

LEFT: Renée Zellweger who plays Ruby in the movie. ABOVE: Iain Smith, executive producer, left, with producer Bill Horberg.

The ground beneath her hands

Scouting Locations

During the early days of pre-production on *Cold Mountain*, deciding where to actually shoot the film took on a particular urgency. Minghella and Ferretti spent the better part of a year, starting in August of 2001, searching for workable locations. At first, the team tried to find a way to shoot the movie in the actual locations where the novel was set. An enormous amount of time was spent in North Carolina, but as hard as the filmmakers tried to use the authentic sites, they faced a serious dilemma.

First, there was the cost of constructing sets. "In the end it turned out that we worked doubly hard," says Minghella, "because we found a whole film's worth of locations in North Carolina, and then had to reevaluate those decisions and look for a more practical way to make the film. Asheville, and its surrounding country, is magnificent but there are very few period buildings and none of them had the characteristics we needed. The cost of extensive building in North Carolina would certainly have exceeded our budget."

Secondly, much of the film needed massive forests for a backdrop but the filmmakers could not find appropriate landscapes in the deep South where filming was permitted. "We kept wondering why the trees in the Carolinas were so small," Dante Ferretti explains. "Eventually we learned this was because of logging practices in the area where trees are cut down every four years. There are no first growth trees left, so the landscape is very different from what it was in the nineteenth century."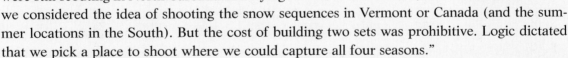

The third important factor to consider was the weather and where to find what they needed. Weather, in fact, plays a significant role in the movie as the story unfolds through the changing of seasons. The story begins in the blazing heat of summer and ends in a monochromatic world, covered in snow. The climax of the movie is played out in a bitter winter storm and the snowy backdrop was crucial to Minghella's vision. "In the past few winters, snowfall in the Asheville region was too unreliable for a film production to gamble on," says Bill Horberg. "There was a period, while we were still scouting in North Carolina and trying to make it work there, that we considered the idea of shooting the snow sequences in Vermont or Canada (and the summer locations in the South). But the cost of building two sets was prohibitive. Logic dictated that we pick a place to shoot where we could capture all four seasons."

Practical considerations had to be kept foremost in mind on a film of this size and scope, and the production team grew more and more concerned about the implications of what it would cost to film the story in North Carolina. It was time to seriously consider other options and to start looking elsewhere.

Though this was a wrenching decision for everyone, ultimately, the year they had spent in

LEFT: The house on Black Cove farm was built from the ground up. ABOVE: The original location for the old mill, shot about a year before construction.

North Carolina proved advantageous. "The fact that we did scout every location in North Carolina and Asheville, in the actual Cold Mountain area where the book is set, was an immensely profitable experience because when we realized that we had to film elsewhere, we left the area with a greater understanding of what had to be re-created," says Minghella.

"Once we gave up on North Carolina, we could look almost anywhere else in the world," says Horberg. "We began casting a wider net than we ever imagined." Their first scheme was to go north, to Canada, the most likely place to find dense forests, or so they thought. It was something of a shock when they discovered that the situation in Canada was quite similar to the one that existed in North Carolina. The Canadian forests are as denatured as those in the United States; furthermore, the variety of trees up north didn't match those in North Carolina's Blue Ridge Mountains.

The filmmakers were uncertain where to look next. Their options were vast; they could look almost anywhere in the civilized world. "We did a lot of research on the internet," explains associate producer Timothy Bricknell. "We were considering Ireland, Poland, and the Pyrennes, among many other places." Executive producer Iain Smith suggested that they consider Romania because he had recently returned from a walking tour of the Carpathian Mountains in Transylvania.

"Making a movie involves finding a balance between art and money," explains Iain Smith. "My task was to protect the money but at the same time to look after the art; to achieve creative freedom within the constraining wall that the money inevitably represents, and to avoid a situation where we just go someplace like Romania simply because it is cheap.

"It is essential to maintain the quality of a movie's vision, especially so in the case of *Cold Mountain*. Miramax couldn't get anywhere near their budget target by shooting in America, and Anthony, somewhat reluctantly, started having to think about Eastern Europe. I was always a strong advocate for shooting in Romania, having visited there the year before. We needed the uncluttered look of nineteenth-century North Carolina, and Romania had those sweeping landscapes that would allow us to make the most of unspoiled scenery through the changing of the seasons, from the heat of summer to the cold of winter.

"Also, we were able to construct sets, using traditional skills, for a mere fraction of what it would have cost elsewhere. We were able to engage the Romanian army for eleven weeks of grueling battle for an astonishing $300,000.

"Of course, these fantastic benefits were still offset by the 'penalty factor' of having to bring in all our key technical crew and facilities from the UK and Italy, but I never doubted that we could pull this off, to the benefit of the movie as a whole.

"We were the first picture of such size to shoot in Romania, and we enjoyed enormous support and flexibility from both Castel Film and the Romanian government. When I wanted to I

could speak directly with the prime minister in Bucharest. For all these reasons I always believed that Romania was the most appropriate place for Anthony to make his movie, and I still hold that view."

Producers Albert Berger and Ron Yerxa, who had first been attracted to the project because of its connection to the Blue Ridge Mountains of North Carolina, were not so ready to be persuaded out of the deep South. They joined the second scouting expedition to see Romania for themselves. "Anthony was very excited about shooting in Romania and the early reports were very promising," says Berger, "but I arrived very, very skeptical. I had had my heart set on North Carolina. However, I had to admit that, of all the locations we had seen, Romania was the first place that felt comparable to North Carolina. It's got a similar feeling, and the landscape featured both the high mountains and the rolling hills that are typical of North Carolina. There were also many unexpected benefits to Romania and it proved to be an ideal location."

Yerxa was equally impressed with Romania. "It's an odd sort of cultural clash being there," he points out, "because you drive through towns that are very old-fashioned and there's a sort of intensity to the quality of life that I think is probably very close to what existed in America in previous centuries."

Overall, it was that fact almost more than anything else—the resemblance of the Romanian

ABOVE: The town of Cold Mountain was constructed from scratch near the town of Zarnesti in a mountain valley of Romania. Minghella says that Dante Ferretti's sets are so authentic that "people will think we just went out and found some old farms."

35

countryside to the nineteenth-century American landscape—that convinced Minghella and his team that they had found their perfect locations. "Romania has hardly experienced an Industrial Revolution in the ways that have permanently transformed Western Europe and North America," Minghella explains. "There is little of the road and rail infrastructure, dense urban development, and deforestation that are features of life in the West. Most of the trees that are felled in Romania are transported by horse and cart. Transylvania is beautiful, primitive, and blessed with huge tracts of unspoiled farmland. It is a country of scratch farming, almost identical to the southern lifestyle Frazier describes in his novel. There were also many opportunities to build sets using local craftsman for whom building in wood is still the vernacular."

So, as unlikely as it may sound to anyone outside of Hollywood, in February of 2002, the decision was finalized: *Cold Mountain*—an authentic historical epic of the American Civil War—would be shot primarily in Eastern Europe.

"In Romania, we could build exactly what we needed for a fraction of the cost of building in the states," explains Sydney Pollack, "and on top of that, we could get a tax benefit. When the numbers get as high as they do with a big-budget movie like *Cold Mountain*, the production budget is really crucial."

Moreover, the lack of modernity in this mountainous country was the visual canvas that had eluded the filmmakers in the United States and Canada. "At once I understood that we could make a film closer to my vision of North Carolina of the 1860s in Romania than we ever could in North Carolina," says Minghella. "We were disappointed, of course, by having to abandon North Carolina but very excited by the opportunities Romania held out for us."

Not long after, the filmmakers discovered that there is a Transylvania county in North Carolina, not far from the actual Cold Mountain. That bit of geographical trivia seemed to underscore the similarity between the two regions—despite their immense distance from each other—and was considered a good omen for the crew.

Once the decision to shoot the film principally in Romania (and on some locations in South Carolina and Virginia) was finalized, Minghella turned his attention more fully to casting—the other crucial element in creating the film he wanted to make.

ABOVE: Photo of the first location scouts in Romania. The Swanger farm will eventually be constructed on this vacant lot of land. RIGHT: Jude Law in one of the film's mountain locations. OVERLEAF: Scenes from the movie of Nicole Kidman and Donald Sutherland shot on the Black Cove Farm location.

like any other thing, a gift

Casting the People of Cold Mountain

I think it's fair to say that as a director, some of the most important work you do is finding the cast," Minghella says. "At the end of the day, no matter how beautiful a costume, location, or particular shot, the single most important element is what happens with an actor. Frankly, I would rather see a wonderful actor standing against a blank wall in poor light than the reverse of that.

"And so I take casting very seriously; it takes me months and months. I meet every actor myself and spend time alone with the person I'm considering for a part. I invest an enormous amount of time because, during the process, I start to figure out the kind of film I want to make—why one actor will fit and another won't. When I cast, I'm already dealing with good actors, so I try and concentrate on the chemistry between us. I think I know what actors I can serve. They, of course, are looking for material, but I'm looking for an environment where they can flourish. In a film like *Cold Mountain*, each important sequence required that a group of people work well with one another so we were not casting one or two people but rather a collection of people."

Most particularly, the film is focused on the interaction between the three main characters: Inman, Ada, and Ruby.

"It was impossible to decide who would play one of those characters without having a sense of all three. I had to define the triangulation in the film," Minghella points out. "In fact I ended up with various permutations so that depending on whether or not this particular person was going to be Inman, then that one could be a potential Ada. And if that person was going to be Ada, then this one might be a potential Ruby. I circled round and round a putative group until I could find a triangle of actors that made the most sense to me."

According to casting director David Rubin, "Anthony's desire to select all three leading performers simultaneously is testament to his understanding that no casting choice should be made in isolation. Casting should never be a matter of filling individual scripted roles with suitable actors, but rather creating a vibrant chemical mixture of personalities, faces, rhythms, and voices in populating an entire ensemble of characters."

Ultimately Minghella decided that Jude Law, Nicole Kidman, and Renée Zellweger would work perfectly together as the embodiment of the heart, mind, and soul of the film. They functioned as a team and each was a crucial element. Synchronicity of these three parts was so important that Minghella waited until he decided on all three of them before offering parts to any one of them. "In fact, the offers to Jude, Nicole, and Renée were made on the same day

like any other thing, a gift

because I felt I couldn't offer a part to any one of them until I knew who I wanted for the other two roles," says Minghella.

In selecting the actors for each of the roles, Minghella examined carefully the characters' contrasting traits. Of Ada and Ruby, he says, "The two women spend a great deal of time together in the film. In some ways the transitions that Ada makes are as much founded upon her relationship with Ruby as they are on her feelings for Inman." Though Ada and Ruby are polar opposites at the start of the film, in coming to terms with each other, they discover a deep similarity in their personalities.

"In a sense, as the story develops, Ada discovers the ground through Ruby and Ruby discovers the air through Ada," Minghella points out. "So I kept thinking I wanted an earth character for Ruby and I wanted an air character for Ada. When I met Nicole I saw this extremely interesting, cerebral woman. But there's also something very grounded about her, which, if suppressed in the beginning of the film, would eventually surface. The same was true for Renée in the sense that while she is extremely grounded, she is also a dreamer with a whimsical inner life."

In Kidman and Zellweger, Minghella discovered two complex, multi-dimensional actresses who could bring depth to their individual characters while simultaneously complimenting each other. In recent years, Nicole Kidman has taken on a stunning variety of roles that have showcased her enormous talents. From her role as Satine in *Moulin Rouge* (2001) to the obsessive Grace in *The Others* (2001), Kidman has shown breathtaking range. In an article Anthony Minghella wrote for *The New York Times* (August 12, 2001), entitled "The House is Dark and the Children Are Afraid," he praised Kidman's work in *The Others*. "Ms. Kidman's wrenching performance, all porcelain and paranoia, strands of sanity stretched to the breaking point, is to this movie what Mr. Nicholson was to *The Shining*, what Catherine Deneuve was to *Repulsion*," he wrote. "Notwithstanding some marvelous work from the supporting cast, this is essentially a monodrama, and Ms. Kidman's gradual fragmentation is heartbreaking."

Add to the mix Kidman's 2002 Academy Award-winning turn as Virginia Woolf in *The Hours* and it becomes obvious that she has been attracted to unconventional roles and has taken enormous risks as an artist. Ada of *Cold Mountain* would challenge the actress in many ways and she was eager to assume the role.

ABOVE: Nicole Kidman and Anthony Minghella on set. RIGHT: Nicole Kidman in the scene where she first meets Renée Zellweger.

This girl I play, Ruby, has been on her own so long she's had to learn to take care of herself and she doesn't waste a lot of time on things that aren't useful. Her hands are always in the dirt, literally. On the other hand, emotion, fine personal relations, they don't have much of a place in her life. She's taught herself how not to feel, how not to express herself. So when she meets a woman who's all about the finer things, who doesn't know how to take care of herself, who can't produce anything of value, she's fascinated and she's affected by knowing her. It's very interesting to play a character affected so deeply by another person and start to open up to another way of living.

–RENÉE ZELLWEGER

"I read the book several years ago when it first came out and was entranced," says Kidman. "The prose is sensory, illusive, and describes the inner life of both Inman and Ada so brilliantly. I thought, how could you ever turn this into a movie? But Anthony is a true poet. He took this magnificent novel and turned it into a fantastic screenplay with its own life.

"Ada is such a wonderful role for a woman. She goes from being a Southern belle who's never had to do anything practical to someone who suddenly has to learn to survive under the most terrible circumstances of war and privation. And I love the theme of female friendship that develops in the story. It's rare that you get two wonderfully rich female roles in the same film."

Like Kidman, Renée Zellweger has also been attracted to very diverse roles from the vulnerable single mom in *Jerry Maguire* (1996) to the lovelorn English girl in *Bridget Jones's Diary* (2001) and the bad-time brawler Roxie Hart in *Chicago* (2002). She, too, shared Kidman's enthusiasm for Charles Frazier's novel.

"I read the book before it was published," says Zellweger. "I have friends who run in the same social circles as the Fraziers in the Carolinas, so I got an early look at the manuscript. It was thrilling to read such a rich account of that period of American history."

LEFT: Renée Zellweger in the scene where Ruby introduces herself to Ada. ABOVE: Minghella, Zellweger, and Kidman in the scene where Ruby and Ada construct a rail fence on Black Cove farm.

I'm very taken with the way Anthony's screenplay
depicts the friendship between Ada and Ruby as something
vibrant, something that survives and conquers, in a way.
The women are polar opposites, and yet instead of being
antagonistic, they teach each other invaluable lessons about
life, they help each other survive. I think this film is very
relevant because of what it says about community
and faith, and about believing in something deeply.

–Nicole Kidman

like any other thing, a gift

From the start, Zellweger believed it would make a terrific film and even helped some independent filmmakers try to obtain the rights. She was eager to become part of the project, playing whatever role she could. In the end, she was delighted when it turned out that Anthony Minghella was going to direct the film and offered her the role of Ruby.

"I know Anthony felt a very strong responsibility to maintain the authenticity and beauty of the book. As for Ruby, I love this girl. She's a survivor, very much of the earth as Anthony says. Her hands are always in the dirt. She knows how to put the seed in the earth and what it's going to produce in the end and when to harvest it. Emotion doesn't play a role in her life, so it's quite fascinating to watch someone like that open up and change."

Having decided on these two formidable actresses for the film, Minghella had to sort out, as he says, who could possible play Inman against them. He had been thinking of Jude Law when he started writing the screenplay but felt reluctant to offer Law the role. "I'd had a wonderful experience with Jude on *Ripley*, and found him a pleasure to work with—willing, very smart, and generous. But I felt he had somehow defined himself as a supporting actor. He'd been very specific in the roles he chose, not only in *Ripley* but in *Road to Perdition* and *A. I.* I sensed a reluctance to take on the weight of carrying a film.

"So my dialogue with Jude was not about whether he could play Inman. I knew he could. Rather, I needed to know if he had the will to endure what anyone playing Inman would have to endure. Eventually, I saw that he did and it was tremendously exciting. I was lucky with Jude in *Ripley*. It was the explosion of somebody fresh in a film, he was a new discovery for so many people. I think the discovery here will be to see him as a romantic leading actor who do can anything on screen."

For his part, Law knew he wanted the role as soon as he read the screenplay.

"I saw immediately that Inman is a role that any actor would die to play," he says. "He is very much an Everyman, the eyes and ears of the audience. At first he's caught up in the excitement and jingoism of the Civil War, believing in the cause of the South. But after enduring the horrors of the war, he embarks on this physical and spiritual journey during which he learns that the only thing worth living for is the love of the woman he is desperately trying to get back to."

ABOVE: Kidman and Zellweger in one of the last scenes in the movie. RIGHT: Donald Sutherland as Reverend Monroe, Ada's father.

Law was also excited about working with Minghella and his crew again. "I'd never done a film with a director a second time, so that was a special pleasure for me. Anthony inspires incredible creativity and incredible calm. The atmosphere on a Minghella film is conducive to everyone for doing his or her best work. I couldn't wait to get started." The producers were equally enthusiastic about casting Jude Law in the role. "We knew from our experience on *Ripley* what a great partner Jude was," says producer Bill Horberg, "how hard he prepared for the role, how much energy he brought into the project, and also how brilliant he was at doing a perfect American accent, which was of course a consideration for Inman."

Although Minghella and the producers had now cast the leading players for the film, the casting process was far from finished. "It's a feature of *Cold Mountain* that by nature the material is episodic—it's the story of a man on a journey and the people he meets along the way. Each encounter is an important encounter," Minghella says. "One thing I've learned as a screenwriter and dramatist is that every single person in a play or screenplay is, at one point or other, a leading character. If, for instance, a waiter comes in and says, 'I'm sorry, the chick-

en is off tonight,' and the camera is on the character as he delivers the line—well, at that moment, he is the leading character. You can't say to the audience, 'Don't pay attention to him, he's not as important as the next person who's about to speak.'"

The action of *Cold Mountain* contains many instances of unforgettable characters who stand center stage briefly in the story, providing opportunities for first rate actors to appear in the film for nine or ten minutes and play, in Minghella's words, "hugely important duets," mostly with Inman

ABOVE: Clockwise from top left: Ray Winstone (Teague); Natalie Portman (Sara); James Gammon (Esco), and Kathy Baker (Sally.)

but also in scenes with Ada and Ruby. "Don't discount one mundane fact—all directors are fans. We want to work with people we admire and have fallen in love with on screen. When I see a great performance in another movie, I covet it. I think, 'I want that kind of performance in my film.' So often casting is just the instinctive delight in the actors skills." With the enthusiasm of any movie fan, Minghella decided he would go after leading actors for what might be considered supporting roles.

"We've got heavyweights in the ring, and we don't want to put a bantam weight to fight opposite them, so to speak. I was looking for someone who—to put it crudely—could punch back as hard as Jude (or Nicole or Renée). I saw the opportunity to cast the film in a way that I'll probably never be able to do again, which is, for example, to call Donald Sutherland for the role of Ada's father; or Eileen Atkins to play Maddy, the goat woman; or Philip Seymour Hoffman for the disgraced minister Veasey; or Natalie Portman as Sara, the helpless farmwoman alone in her cabin with her sickly child; or Giovanni Ribisi for Junior, the backwoodsman who keeps a bevy of women and brood of children in his shack."

Call them Minghella did, and cast them he did, along with other stellar actors. "This period

was about reaching out. One of the marvelous things about casting is you start to accumulate a team and then other actors want to join those people," says the director. "The truth is that all these actors are valued by their peers." In the end, Minghella, in conjunction with casting directors David Rubin and Ronna Kress, gathered together an extraordinary ensemble of actors: Ray Winstone (*Sexy Beast*) as Teague, the murderous head of the Home Guard; Brendan Gleeson (*Gangs of New York*) as Stobrod, the iterant fiddler who turns out to be

CLOCKWISE FROM TOP LEFT: Brendan Gleeson (Stobrod); Eileen Atkins (Maddy); Jena Malone (Ferry Girl); Charles Hunnam (Bosie).

Ruby's father; Kathy Baker (*Cider House Rules*) and James Gammon (*Life, Or Something Like It*) as Sally and Esco Swanger, Ada's neighbors and Cold Mountain Town elders who oppose the war; Charlie Hunnam (*Nicholas Nickleby*) as Bosie, a dark angel who is Teague's murderous associate; Ethan Suplee (*Remember the Titans*) as Pangle, Stobrod's goodhearted but simple musical companion; Jena Malone (*Life as a House*) as the Ferry Girl on the Cape Fear River; Melora Walters (*Magnolia*) as Junior's lusty wife Lila; Jack White of the rock group White Stripes in his film debut as Georgia, a musician who travels with Stobrod and Pangle; and Lucas Black (*Sling Blade*) as Oakley, a youthful recruit from Cold Mountain Town's Civil War regiment.

"Although this is essentially an American story," explains David Rubin, "the casting process today ideally should involve a global perspective, especially given the increasing ability of English-speaking actors worldwide to adopt an American dialect and vernacular. Anthony's openness to actors of all nationalities resulted in our assembling literally the 'best of all worlds' on screen."

"The film works on a very large canvas with a lot of great actors in very meaty roles, and we've got not only seasoned veterans but so many of today's most interesting, wonderful young performers," says producer Albert Berger.

"I was so fortunate," Minghella adds. "I've got an amazing cast for this film. I pushed hard, right to the edges, and was able to get everyone I wanted. It was really a blessing."

Now that the director had his townspeople and his landscape, he needed someone to build him a town.

LEFT: Philip Seymour Hoffman (Veasey) and Giovanni Ribisi (Junior). ABOVE: Clockwise from top left: Melora Walters (Lila); Ethan Suplee (Pangle); Jack White (Georgia), and Lucas Black (Oakley).

The shadow of a crow

Production Design

By any measure, Dante Ferretti is among the world's leading and most sought-after production designers. Ferretti has worked with the most formidable directors of his generation: Federico Fellini, Pier Paolo Pasolini, Martin Scorsese, Franco Zeffirelli, Neil Jordan, Martin Brest, and Jean-Jacques Annaud, among many others. Minghella, like many other directors working today, had wanted to work with Ferretti for a long time.

"Ferretti is very dedicated, there wasn't a day when he wasn't at the set worrying or working. No detail was too small or insignificant for him. What he has done for this film cannot be overestimated," Minghella says, "but I fear that he has done such a good job that his work will go unnoticed. The work is so authentic and true to the time period that people will see the movie and think we just went out and found some old farms. The reality is that every single building, with the exception of some street shots in Charleston, was built and designed by Dante."

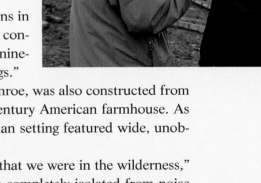

In the hills of Romania, in a place called Poiana Brasov, Ferretti constructed (from scratch!) more than thirty-two buildings along a stretch of dirt road in order to create the town of Cold Mountain. His town included a church and a graveyard, a general store, a rooming house, stables, a laundry, a bank—even a dentist's office. In every shot, the town teems with life and every single detail of the construction was authentic.

"Everything we built was based on research we did on towns in the Blue Ridge and Smoky Mountains," Ferretti says. "We constructed the buildings as they would have been built in the nineteenth century—everything is made entirely of rough-hewn logs."

The Black Cove Farm, home of the Reverend and Ada Monroe, was also constructed from the ground up. It was conceived as a traditional nineteenth-century American farmhouse. As would have been true of that time period, the remote Romanian setting featured wide, unobstructed vistas.

"The beauty of shooting on these Romanian locations was that we were in the wilderness," says Ferretti. "Black Cove Farm and Cold Mountain Town are completely isolated from noise and modern life and I was able to construct them so that the camera could film from a 360 degree perspective without having to avoid anything that would violate the period. For me, the greatest satisfaction is that although it matches the landscape of North Carolina perfectly, it's wilder, richer, more primitive, and it perfectly re-creates the feeling of nineteenth-century America."

LEFT: Detail from an illustration by Dante Ferretti of the Black Cove Farm. Ferretti's incredible illustrations measure 30 by 80 inches. ABOVE: Ferretti and Bill Horberg on location in Romania. OVERLEAF: Detail from a Ferretti illustration of the scene in the town of Cold Mountain where Inman marches off to war.

ABOVE: Scouting shot of the location where the town of Cold Mountain will be constructed in Romania. BELOW RIGHT: Anthony Minghella during the construction of the town. BELOW: Crew members take a break during construction. OPPOSITE PAGE: Detail of the completed town of Cold Mountain as it appears in the film.

ABOVE: Detail from an illustration by Dante Ferretti of an overview of Junior's farm. RIGHT: Interior drawing of Junior's cabin by Ferretti. BELOW: The cabin as it appears in the movie. OVERLEAF: Interior shot of Junior's cabin during filming. From left: Jude Law (Inman); Katherine Durio (Mae); Philip Seymour Hoffman (Veasey); Taryn Manning (Shyla); Melora Walters (Lila), and Giovanni Ribisi (Junior.)

JUNIOR
I'd like to propose a toast: to
the last toast! He's gone now.
Look! His eyes have gone.

INMAN (*vaguely, drunk*)
What?

JUNIOR
I'm leaving soon as I'm full.

VEASEY
Really. Goodbye.

JUNIOR
Got a bunch of traps needs
visiting. I'll be back tomorrow,
before dark. You'll still be here?

VEASEY
That's my fervent prayer.

Inman gets up suddenly, sways.

INMAN
I'll say my good-byes, got miles
and miles to go before I reach
the Blue Ridge. (*head spinning*)
I'll just quickly lie down. This
house is on a bit of a tilt.

And he stumbles over to the fire
where he instantly curls up.

VEASEY
I'm heading for that smoke-
house and I'm ready to be
washed clean of my dirt.

LEFT: *Detail from a Dante Ferretti illustration of Black Cove farm. ABOVE: The farm under construction in Romania. BELOW: Nicole Kidman stands in front of the finished farm house as it appears in the film.*

jacket ①

skirt

bodice

trim &
jacket

insertion

Ann Roth is not simply
putting costumes on actors,
she's also making character.

–ANTHONY MINGHELLA

COLD MOUNT
Ann Roth

ashes of roses

Costumes

In any movie, but especially a period piece, the costumes are an essential contribution to defining and explaining the character in a kind of visual shorthand. Ann Roth's costumes for *Cold Mountain* are no exception.

Roth has the director's complete trust. "Costume design is the one area of the film where I do not interfere at all," Minghella says. "I leave it entirely up to Ann because I know there is nothing that I can contribute that would be better than what she can come up with. After working with her, the actors often learn more about their character, about how they might play a part. Ann really understands each character in ways that I could not articulate."

Authenticity in design, fabric and color dyes are a hallmark of Roth's work. Indeed, Roth has very strong ideas about what the characters should be wearing—and why. "I've designed several films set in nineteenth-century America and have steeped myself in the period," she says.

Roth's costumes are authentic right down to the underwear. Literally. For *Cold Mountain* Roth insisted that the actors wear actual nineteenth-century underwear, or underwear made according to nineteenth-century patterns. "It helps them walk properly," she explains.

Renée Zellweger agrees. "Everything I had on right down to the buttons and fastenings and buckles was period," says the actress. "As for the underwear—it took a good half hour to go the ladies room because of the fastenings. There were no shortcuts with this clothing, no elastic waistbands. You stand a little differently wearing it. There's no ease to the clothing. It's definitely part of the hands-on, hard life. Everything is about function, and it's a big part of this character."

Of course, the costumes for Ada were more elaborate than those for Ruby. In fact, Ada's wardrobe is more varied than that of any other character in the movie. At the start of the story Ada wears custom-tailored, flowing dresses made of silks and satins, lacy stockings and fancy-heeled shoes, all accessorized by extraordinary hats. Roth designed each of these outfits, working closely with Kidman and Minghella as the costumes took shape.

But as time goes by—after Inman leaves and her father dies—Ada's wardrobe begins to deteriorate. The fancy veiled hats disappear. The elaborate dresses become dirty and then threadbare. Eventually her silks and satins disintegrate all together, much like the life she once lived in Cold Mountain.

"Her clothes just fall away," Roth says. "In a way, her character evolves piece by piece and you can see it by what she wears." As she seems to go mad from grief and loneliness, Ada can barely dress herself. She wears her father's old coat over her bodice. By the end of the movie,

ABOVE: Costume designer Ann Roth and producer Sydney Pollack in Romania. LEFT: Ann Roth's sketches for the dresses worn by Nicole Kidman and Kathy Baker, as shown in inset.

however, Ada has become another person. She wears pants and boots; her clothes are a true reflection of her evolution from frail and incompetent to sensible and self-sufficient.

Much more basic, but no less important, are Inman's clothes.

"Inman's on the move and he doesn't really change clothing," says Roth. "The most important thing was for his clothes to give weight to his character. After all, Inman's a brooding, heroic man, the pivotal figure in this epic, and what he wears has to reflect that. His vest, shirt, trousers—even his hat— they're traditional clothes from the period, earth-colored, basic with no frills. The clothes echo the character's strength."

The villainous Teague is also dressed to reveal his character. "Teague is strong but much more menacing than Inman. He's taken the law into his own hands and his clothes reflect that. He's in dark earth tones but we gave him a signature piece of clothing to mark him as different—a greatcoat made from an oilskin fabric. The coat creates a renegade look for the character."

For the soldier's costumes, Roth worked closely with Dan Troiani, who served on the production as the Civil War uniform and equipage consultant. Troiani is one of the foremost authorities on Civil War memorabilia, uniforms, and artifacts and has been collecting these items for many years.

Roth examined Troiani's collection closely and studied Mathew Brady photographs from the era. What emerged from her extensive research was that, whereas the Northern soldiers had a standard look for their

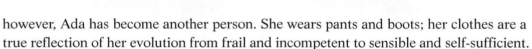

LEFT: Ann Roth sketch for Maddy's costume, as shown in the photo of Eileen Atkins (Maddy). CENTER: Sketches for dresses of Ruby (Zellweger). Inset photos: Top: detail from the sleeve of Ruby's dress. Below: Detail of the cuff of Ruby's pants. RIGHT: Ann Roth sketches for other dresses worn by Sally Swanger and Ada.

Bodice #8

AR
02

69

It's a huge task to take a character that has been so beautifully rendered in a novel and decide what she should be in the film. You say to yourself, "Well, there she is, she's mapped out, but now I have to make her breathe. I have to give her a heart and make her exist in the world."

—NICOLE KIDMAN

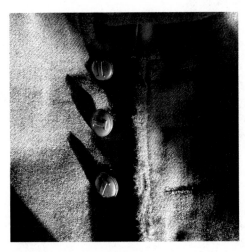

uniform—dark blue jacket, light blue trousers—the Confederate army was a more motley group, with ragtag uniforms that varied from state to state, the accent for the most part being on earth colors and different shades of grey. In re-creating the distinctive look of the uniforms of the period, Roth made the decision to create the costumes from fabric that was similar to the kind used during the Civil War.

"I found people in the Amish country who wove fabric in the old-fashioned way, using very old fiber. I was even able to locate a few original fabrics that date from the era," Roth says. "When making the uniforms for the film, we also used original patterns from the period. We brought everything we had collected in America with us to Romania where Carlo Poggioli, my associate designer, set up a factory in the town of Rasnov to make the costumes."

One problem Roth and her crew faced was how to replicate the distinctive color of the actual Civil War uniforms. Modern dyes were out of the question—the colors would never look authentic to the period.

"We couldn't do real dyes from the past," explains Roth. "In the old days, dyes were made from berries and walnuts. That technology is impractical to re-create. But using modern techniques we tried to capture the true nature of the color of the costumes as they looked 140 years ago. We worked carefully, and I think we succeeded."

The success of Roth's costume designs and her contribution to the film is perhaps best summed up by the director who notes, "Ann is not simply putting costumes on actors, she's also making character."

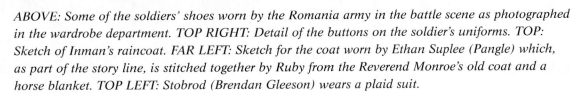

ABOVE: Some of the soldiers' shoes worn by the Romania army in the battle scene as photographed in the wardrobe department. TOP RIGHT: Detail of the buttons on the soldier's uniforms. TOP: Sketch of Inman's raincoat. FAR LEFT: Sketch for the coat worn by Ethan Suplee (Pangle) which, as part of the story line, is stitched together by Ruby from the Reverend Monroe's old coat and a horse blanket. TOP LEFT: Stobrod (Brendan Gleeson) wears a plaid suit.

the doing of it

The color of despair

The Battle of the Crater

Scheduling the actual production of *Cold Mountain* began with one huge question: When should we shoot the battle scene?

"There were some who felt we should wait several weeks before we attempted the most ambitious and formidable element in the film," Minghella explains. "But my fear was that if we did, our attention would have been off—we would still be preparing for the battle scene while we worked on something else."

"Our original plan was to shoot the winter scenes first and end with the big battle scene," says Bill Horberg. "But the logistics of production dictated that we start with the battle scene because it was the most expensive shoot in the film and would require the largest crew base. If we shot this sequence first, we could then wind down the size of the crew."

For these and other practical reasons, the production team decided to start with the battle sequence. Before long, Minghella began to see this scene as a separate, short film that would be made prior to shooting the actual film. "We had crew members who only worked during the battle film," says the director. "We used additional props and effects and an additional camera department in order to give us the kind of resources we would need just for this scene."

As if the scheduling and the logistics of a three-week shoot that involved thousands of extras and tons of explosives were not enough, the battle scene represented another enormous challenge for Anthony Minghella. "We wanted to avoid the sense of reenactment that turns up in most films of the Civil or Revolutionary War," explains Horberg. "We wanted a quality of first-time authenticity and nonvarnished life that didn't feel like it came out of the Smithsonian Museum."

Minghella claims that his greatest advantage was his inexperience. "Every director has to know that when doing a scene like this, you are up against all the other remarkable scenes that have already been done. I felt that, if I had any strength at all, it was because I did not know what I was doing. I am not a veteran director of action sequences and because I do not have that experience, my hope was that I could make this scene more human."

Preparations for this daunting undertaking began months before the actual shoot and consumed the crew. Describing

LEFT: Tintype image created by photographer Stephen Berkman of Jude Law (Inman), Jay Tavare (Swimmer), Lucas Black (Oakley), Trey Howell (Butcher), and Ben Allison (Rourke). ABOVE: The filmmakers shooting a battle scene: Jude Law (far left); John Seale, director of photography (wearing a white hat), and Anthony Minghella (seated, far right).

the work in his journal, Anthony Minghella wrote: "The Battle at Petersburg is the most choreographed and prepared scene of the film. When you are preparing a battle sequence, you are preparing a small battle yourself, you must approach it with the clearest strategy and most transparent method."

And so, on July 15, 2002, almost five years after Minghella first read Charles Frazier's novel, on a tract of farmland on the outskirts of Bucharest, the *Cold Mountain* team began filming one of the most ferocious battles ever fought on American soil.

This famous Civil War battle, known as the Battle of the Crater, took place on July 30, 1864, in Petersburg, Virginia. The battle, only briefly outlined in Frazier's novel, is transformed into a key scene in Minghella's screenplay. "I didn't ever want this to be a Civil War film but I wanted one event, one

LEFT: The Romanian army prepares to reenact the Battle of the Crater. At the bottom of the photo, far right, John Seale, director of photography (in the white hat) and Minghella (speaking into a megaphone). ABOVE: Detail of the production shooting down into the crater. OVERLEAF: Detail of a Dante Ferretti drawing of the battle scene.

79

Am I Born to Die

And am I born to die
To lay this body down
And must my trembling spirit fly
Into a world unknown

And my trembling spirit fly
Into a world unknown

A land of deepest shade
Unpierced by human fault
That prairie region of the dead
Where all things are forgot

Soon as from Earth I go
What will become of me
Eternal happiness of woe
Must then my portion be

*Stobrod plays this song at the start of the film,
when Oakley dies during the Battle of the
Crater. It is played in a choral arrangement
over the battlefield.*

battle, that demonstrated the medieval and high-tech nature of the conflict. Weapons were becoming powerful in the 1860s but field strategies were antiquated. Military structure had not yet caught up with the power of modern weapons. I wanted to conjure these particular characteristics so that when Inman runs away we understand that it is not from lack of heroism. He needed to be both physically sick and sick of battle," Minghella says.

Minghella chose to illustrate this particular battle because it was an apt example of the sheer brutality and futility of war, an appropriate summation of Inman's four years of fighting. By any measure, the battle was an unnerving event; even for seasoned soldiers who had been at war for many years. Historical letters and journal entries from the men who witnessed and participated in the battle describe it as "the day of Satan in human form."

The battle was part of General Grant's strategy to capture the town of Petersburg, the supply depot for Richmond, as the first step in taking Richmond itself. The specific plan involved tunneling under the Confederate lines at Petersburg, blowing a hole in the earth underneath the enemy and then making a surprise siege on the stunned Southern army. Unfortunately, the tactic backfired. The crater blasted by the Federals was so enormous that when their own troops surged forward, in the smoke and confusion, they fell into the pit and then became trapped. The Confederates gathered their forces and bore down on them. What followed was human slaughter on an unimaginable scale.

In the Minghella screenplay, Inman witnesses the initial carnage, fights bravely during the battle, rescues the mortally wounded Oakley (Lucas Black), one of his Cold Mountain Town compatriots, and then gets seriously wounded himself while on a nighttime reconnaissance mission with Swimmer (Jay Tavare), the Cherokee scout.

A key element of the battle and its aftermath was Dante Ferretti's extraordinary set, a painstaking re-creation of the original site that brought to life the battlefield in all its horrify-

ing glory. "I went to Petersburg in Virginia to visit the historic battlefield because I wanted to get a true sense of the place, feel exactly what it was like and get a grasp on all the details," Ferretti says. "I was interested in seeing the quality of the light there, to get a sense exactly of the position of the sun at the start of the battle, where shadows were cast, and what the sky looked like later in the day, too."

On the large expanse of farmland in Potigrafu near Bucharest which the filmmakers rented from local farmers, Ferretti and his crew dug trenches, laid railroad tracks, built fortifications and embankments, and even constructed a makeshift army hospital. Most notably, Ferretti and his crew re-created the battle's huge crater, a hole that replicated the original, measuring from 30 to 50 deep feet deep in different places to approximately 170 feet long and 60 to 80 feet wide. A smaller crater was also constructed for close-up footage.

The blast, which in fact signals the start of the battle, was engineered by Trevor Wood, special effects technician on the film. Wood used 4,000 liters of petrol, 100 kilograms of high explosive, and a quantity of pyrotechnics positioned on steel plates on the ground in a mixture that also included sand, dirt, wood chippings, and bits of bark. The pyrotechnics, material ordinarily used to make fireworks, was added primarily to create the explosion's fireball.

Minghella and Seale used four cameras to film the blast, and got it in one take.

Above all, Minghella was after a heightened realism in the scene—a sense of verisimilitude that was crucial in the creation of the actual time and place of the battle.

Three military and historical advisers, Brian Pohanka, John Bert, and Michael Kraus, served as technical advisers. "Anthony wanted the battle to be as authentic as possible, especially as it was something that wasn't especially featured in the novel. He wanted every detail to be correct," Pohanka says.

ABOVE: Three shots from the opening scene in the movie, the great explosion that starts the Battle of the Crater. Photos by Michelle Pizanis. The battle scene was re-created from historical documents and archival illustrations from the period. LEFT: Interior shot of the Confederate soldiers before the battle begins. OVERLEAF: Detail from a Dante Ferretti illustration of the battle sequence.

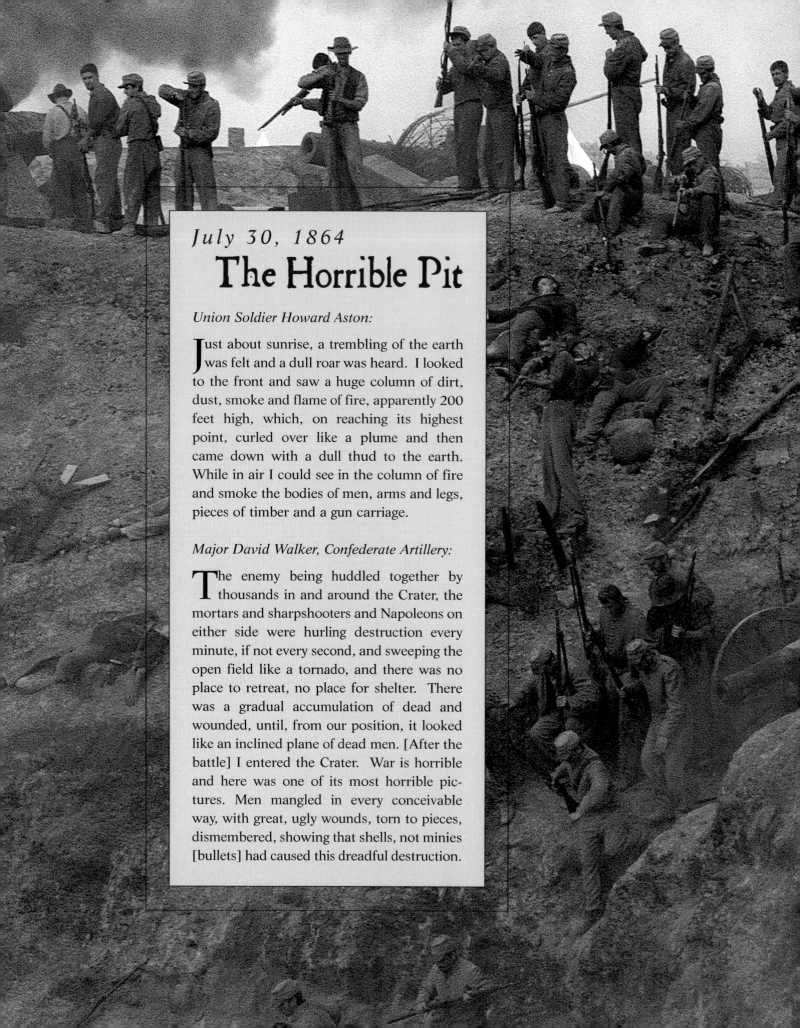

July 30, 1864
The Horrible Pit

Union Soldier Howard Aston:

Just about sunrise, a trembling of the earth was felt and a dull roar was heard. I looked to the front and saw a huge column of dirt, dust, smoke and flame of fire, apparently 200 feet high, which, on reaching its highest point, curled over like a plume and then came down with a dull thud to the earth. While in air I could see in the column of fire and smoke the bodies of men, arms and legs, pieces of timber and a gun carriage.

Major David Walker, Confederate Artillery:

The enemy being huddled together by thousands in and around the Crater, the mortars and sharpshooters and Napoleons on either side were hurling destruction every minute, if not every second, and sweeping the open field like a tornado, and there was no place to retreat, no place for shelter. There was a gradual accumulation of dead and wounded, until, from our position, it looked like an inclined plane of dead men. [After the battle] I entered the Crater. War is horrible and here was one of its most horrible pictures. Men mangled in every conceivable way, with great, ugly wounds, torn to pieces, dismembered, showing that shells, not minies [bullets] had caused this dreadful destruction.

the color of despair

Using that as his mandate, Pohanka made certain even the smallest details were on target. "The troops that dug the tunnel under the Confederate lines were from the 48th Regiment, which was from a coal mining area in Pennsylvania, so of course they knew what they were doing. I made sure that we put a number 48 on the caps of the soldiers from the regiment since the camera sees them up close.

"Later, at the end of the battle, a Confederate soldier picks up a bloodied fragment of a flag from the 100th Pennsylvania Regiment. It's a documented incident and we included it. Anthony particularly liked the reality of the Confederate picking up the flag," Pohanka says.

"Our job was to train the soldiers in the nineteenth-century tactics and drills that the Civil War troops actually used in battle," says John Bert. "The way Civil War soldiers held their weapons is very different from the way soldiers do it today. The manner of deploying them evolved from the Napoleonic drill. Each move was set down in a manual called *Hardee's Light Infantry Tactics*. They involved the shoulder arms, the right shoulder shift, and the bayonet charge. The weapons were heavier, longer, and more unwieldy than those used by modern soldiers.

"These elaborate tactics of the drill was one reason for the disaster. The technology of weaponry had evolved more quickly than tactics, and the Federals, screaming and charging aggressively into the pit, bayonets thrust forward, weren't prepared for the onslaught of the Confederates on top of them."

Rather than hire extras, the production obtained the services of the Romanian Armed Forces, employing over a thousand Romanian servicemen, including more than 200 paratroopers, all of whom were divided into Federal and Confederate troops.

The Romanian soldiers responded with great enthusiasm to what they were asked to do for the film. Even though the weapons were new to them, after practice they executed the moves with precision and exactitude. "What's more, they looked right for their role in the film. Romanian soldiers are much younger and thinner than their American counterparts," Pohanka says. "And in that respect they really resemble what soldiers looked like in the Civil War. Soldiers then were much more gaunt than Americans are today."

The three weeks it took to film the battle and its aftermath were not nearly as horrific as the actual battle itself, of course, but they were arduous on their own terms. The weather didn't cooperate (a condition that persisted for much of the work in Romania), and scenes were filmed in either blazing, 100-degree heat or, even worse, in pouring rain. The constant downpour created extremely muddy conditions, transforming the battlefield into a mucky, sluggish, and slippery mess. (Every evening, the cast and crew returned to their hotel completely covered in mud; management at the Bucharest Marriott pleaded with them to remove their shoes and muddiest pieces of outer clothing, at the very least, before entering the hotel lobby.)

Once the battlefield sequence was completed, the unit packed up and departed Bucharest. They traveled more than a hundred miles north to the town of Poiana Brasov in Transylvania, a part of the country referred to as the Transylvanian Alps (actually the Carpathian mountain range) where all of the other location filming in Romania was going to take place.

"At the end of this short film," Minghella comments, "we made a whole movie."

ABOVE TOP: Anthony Minghella videotaping the scale model of the battlefield created by production designer Dante Ferretti. The model was more than 15 feet long and included toy soldiers to show the placement of actors. ABOVE: Details from a scale model. RIGHT: Scenes from the Battle of the Crater sequence.

Hell has busted!

What he told Veasey was about the blowup at Petersburg. His regiment had been situated directly beside the South Carolina boys that got exploded by the Federal tunnelers. Inman was in the wattled trenches parching rye to make a pot of what they would call coffee when the ground heaved up along the lines to his right. A column of dirt and men rose into the air and then fell all around. Inman was showered with dirt. A piece of a man's lower leg with the boot still on the foot landed right beside him. A man down the trench from Inman came running through and hollering, Hell has busted!

The men in the trenches to left and right of the hole fell back expecting an attack, but in a little while they realized that the Federals had rushed into the crater and then, amazed at what they had done, just huddled there, confused by that new landscape of pure force.

Right quick Haskell called up his éprouvette mortars and put them just beyond the lip of the crater and had them loaded with a scant ounce and a half of powder, since all they had to do was loft the shells fifty feet to where the Federals milled about like a pen of shoats waiting for the hammer between the eyes. The mortar fire blew many of them to pieces, and when that was done, Inman's regiment led the attack into the crater, and the fighting inside was of a different order from any he had done before. It was war in its most antique form, as if hundreds of men were put into a cave, shoulder to shoulder, and told to kill each other. There was no room for firing and loading muskets, so they mainly used them as clubs. Inman saw one little drummer boy beating a man's head in with an ammunition box. The Federals hardly even bothered to fight back. All underfoot were bodies and pieces of bodies, and so many men had come apart in the blowup and the shelling that the ground was slick and threw a terrible stink from their wet internalments. The raw dirt walls of the crater loomed all around with just a circle of sky above, as if this was all the world there was and fighting was all there was to it. They killed everybody that didn't run away.

—CHARLES FRAZIER, FROM HIS NOVEL

exile and brute wandering

Filming in the Transylvanian Alps

On August 5, 2002, filming began on a wide stretch of mountain valley land near the town of Rasnov. Here Ferretti had constructed from the ground up the Black Cove Farm, a traditional nineteenth-century American farmhouse surrounded by fertile fields, stables, barns, outhouses, slave quarters, a corn crib, and flower gardens. In Minghella's script, Black Cove Farm once belonged to the character Teague's forebears (a plot twist that was not in the original novel). As in the novel, though, the Reverend Monroe (Donald Sutherland) and his daughter, Ada, have moved to Cold Mountain from Charleston and purchased the farm because the Reverend is about to become the head of the congregation in town.

Minghella shot several scenes at the farm to capture the landscape at the height of summer including, most importantly, the social gathering inside the Monroe parlor during which Ada plays the piano and sings, greets her guests and offers them lemonade. The guests at the gathering also include Teague (Ray Winstone) and his associates who identify themselves as outsiders in the community. Inman, who arrives late, stands outside on the porch, drenched with rain, looking longingly through the window at Ada. She finds an excuse to join him on the porch, carrying a tray of drinks.

Scenes of the Reverend and Ada taking Inman on a tour of their farm were also shot here, as well as those depicting the death of Reverend Monroe and shots of Ada alone in the house after her father's death.

Leaving Black Cove, the unit then moved to an another important location in the area of Poiana Brasov, this one somewhat more distant than Black Cove Farm, an hour's drive in the opposite direction. Near the town of Zarnesti, in another Romanian mountain valley, Ferretti built the entire community called Cold Mountain Town.

Several of the film's opening scenes (the back story) were shot here, including Inman's first encounter with Ada, as he is perched on the rafters of the chapel that he and several other young townsmen are building. This is the scene where Ada and Inman speak to each other for the first time, thanks to the intervention of Sally Swanger (Kathy Baker). "If you would just a say a word to one of these fools," Sally says to Ada, "I could get my top field cleared."

Summer scenes set in Cold Mountain Town were filmed inside the completed chapel, one in which Ada finds herself alone with Inman, and another during which the entire congregation

learns that war has been declared. Teague and his men ominously announce that they are the Home Guard, a kind of civilian peace-keeping posse.

Next shot was the sequence inside Inman's rooming house where Ada presents him with a farewell gift, a book and a tintype of herself. "I'm not smiling in it," she explains in Minghella's screenplay. "I don't know how to do that, hold a smile, so now I'm solemn." Moved by the gesture, Inman surprises her with a kiss. Then he must hurry off to join his retreating regiment. Marching

off to war, he glances back, taking one long last look over his shoulder at Ada. She is seen leaning over the top floor railing on the balcony, straining to find him in the crowd.

Major scenes completed at Cold Mountain Town, the unit next moved to yet another farmstead, the Swanger Farm, home of Sally and Esco Swanger (James Gammon), that Ferretti created on the outskirts of

so much death

Inman had seen so much death it had come to seem a random thing entirely. He could not even make a start at reckoning up how many deaths he had witnessed of late. It would number, no doubt, in the thousands. Accomplished in every custom you could imagine, and some you couldn't come up with if you thought at it for days. He had grown so used to seeing death, walking among the dead, sleeping among them, numbering himself calmly as among the near-dead, that it seemed no longer dark and mysterious. He feared his heart had been touched by the fire so often he might never make a civilian again.

—CHARLES FRAZIER, FROM HIS NOVEL

Poiana Brasov. Here Minghella shot one of the most lyrical moments in the movie. Ada sits in a moving cart, playing her treasured piano, as a bare-chested Inman, plowing the Swanger's field, stands transfixed by the haunting image.

The change of seasons that are portrayed on Black Cove Farm, and the contrast in the landscape between Inman's travels and the life the women are leading at home, play an important role in the fabric of the film and represented a major challenge for John Seale, the director of photography. Capturing the look of the different seasons on film was sometimes difficult to control on location, especially given the volatility and unpredictability of conditions in Romania.

Seale had of course previously shot outdoors for Minghella on both *The English Patient* and *The Talented Mr. Ripley*, on locations as different and varied as the rolling Tuscan hills, the windswept Sahara, and the narrow, winding canals on the streets of Venice. He felt prepared for any eventuality on *Cold Mountain*. Some days, however, the wild mood swings of the weather in Transylvania presented him with unexpected problems.

"John has had to cope with such vagaries of weather and he's done it with such alacrity and skill," Minghella says. "When we did *The English Patient*, he weathered a really hard shoot but we also had the luxury of shooting in a studio some of the time. Here we didn't have that luxury. We were always outside in rain, in blazing, blazing heat, under clouds that appeared to hang in for hours when we needed sun, and bright, bright sunlight when we needed clouds, not to mention the disappearing light when the winter sun started to set at four P.M. Yet somehow John managed to keep us shooting day after day without a break."

Seale himself is quite matter-of-fact about the situation. "Shooting exteriors is always a challenge because the weather has a hold of you as opposed to a soundstage where you can create your own weather. In addition, we had to deal with filming in mountains and canyons, which make short days even shorter. In the mountains it is sometimes nine in the morning before the sun comes over the edge and it starts setting before you're even aware of it. Shooting as we have done in deep forests also affects the light. So it's a constant battle. I use high-speed negative film and we work as quickly as we can."

An even bigger challenge for Seale was to establish the contrast in the film, not between time periods but in the physical distances between the leading characters.

"Unlike *The English Patient*, we're not shooting flashback. The characters are all experiencing the same chronological time. It's just that they're hundreds of miles away from each other. Cutting from bright sunshine to overcast and gray can be too sudden for viewers. In reality, at any given time it can be raining in one place and sunny 300 miles away but, in a film, such shifts can be jarring. In the film Inman is climbing a mountain in the muck and the rain and at the same moment Ada's planting potatoes in the late afternoon sun. So you work out subtle ways to make the transitions less stark so that the sense of time flows the same way through both scenes and the visual doesn't call attention to itself. Other times you want a strong contrast between night and day to underline the distance between the characters."

Another complicating factor was that Seale had to re-create the look of the nineteenth century. For this he referred to historical documents and art. "We did a lot of research and looked at Mathew Brady photographs from the era and paintings by Winslow Homer, and lesser-known figures such as Andrew McCallum and Tom Lovell, especially for the battle scenes," says Seale. "The battle of Petersburg was marked by this massive explosion. A pall of burnt gunpowder hung over the crater. Paintings of the battle depict how the smoke permeated the atmosphere, so I went a little wild in the scene with tobacco reds and similarly colored filters to get the look of burnt sienna, the feeling that the place was thick with burnt gunpowder and blood and dirt.

ABOVE: Director of photography John Seale. LEFT: Kathy Baker (Sally Swanger) on location at the Swanger farm.

**INT. BLACK COVE FARM. NIGHT.
WINTER 1863**

Ada is writing. A lonely room. She touches
her father's prayerbook. Grieving.

> ADA (V. O.)
> —I'm still waiting, as I promised,
> I would—

**EXT. BLACK COVE FARM. DAY.
WINTER 1863**

A strong wind, winter. Ada bent double
in the gale as she tries to coax a cow into
the barn.

> ADA (V. O.)
> —but I find myself alone, and at the
> end of my wits—

**INT. HOSPITAL, CHARLESTON.
NIGHT. SUMMER 1864**

Mrs. Morgan reads to Inman, trying to
decipher the letter:

> MRS. MORGAN
> —at the end of my wits, so now I say to
> you, plain as I can, come back to me.

**EXT. BLACK COVE FARM. DAY.
WINTER 1863**

> ADA (V. O.)
> Come back to me is my request.

Come back to me is my request.

"But overall we didn't want to push too hard in this stylized direction. We decided to go fairly clean as a motion picture. I decided to use two different negative stocks. One has a little more contrast for the scenes in which Inman is traveling so the hardships he endures are depicted very clearly.

"We used a softer negative stock for some the scenes at the end of the film and for those scenes with Ada and Ruby on Black Cove farm, no matter the season. We decided to use only sources of light as they were in the 1860s—from daylight, sunlight, cloud, moonlight, and ambient night light, candles, oil lamps, and fires."

Along with his longtime associate, chief lighting technician Morris Flam, Seale worked out a system to enhance these simple sources of light. "We came up with the idea of using hidden light bulbs to emulate candles, to create little pools of light here and there around the room," Flam says. "We didn't want it to look incongruous. We wanted to enhance the light but keep a realistic ambience so that the audience believed they were watching something that occurred during the time frame of the film. And it worked."

Apparently, the director agreed. Minghella is generous in his evaluation of Seale's skills and his contribution to the making of the film. He says, "Legend is that most directors of photography are quite slow, with the cast and crew waiting around for the DP to finish lighting. With John it is almost the reverse. He's always ready and often waiting for everyone else to catch up. I can't imagine making this film with anyone else."

Despite the problems of capturing the light in the mountain valleys of Eastern Europe,

after more than six weeks of shooting among the glorious landscapes and amazing sets of the Swanger and Black Cove farms, the advantages of making the film in Romania were clear to everyone. A sense prevailed that the unit existed in a Romanian world parallel to the very world and time of the story Minghella was telling, a situation that couldn't help but inform the film with a certain richness and texture.

In the scene at the Swangers farm, for instance, "Jude is pushing a hand plow led by a horse as he tills the field, and he's holding the plow in one hand and the horse's reins with the other," Minghella says. "The plow is made of wood and resembles a kind of medieval contraption, but it's absolutely authentic.

"The extraordinary thing is that driving to work every morning through the countryside we would pass any number of Romanian scratch farms where farmers were working with similar antiquated machinery. We saw them cutting down grass, not with tractors or other modern farm equipment, but by hand with scythes. On the road, we would pass farmers transporting their harvest by horse and wooden cart. The marvelous thing was that it felt as if we were actually in the nineteenth century. There was no dislocation between the world we tried to create and the world we inhabited. The actors felt it as well, and it added to their sense of what we were creating."

Jude Law agrees. "There was a certain remoteness there, a wonderful kind of rural simplicity to the countryside and a refreshing lack of urbanization," he explains. "Everything was so unspoiled, we could absolutely surrender to the period. It made such a difference, driving

Ada examined the girl further. She was a dark thing, corded through the neck and arms. Frail-chested. Her hair was black and coarse as a horse's tail. Broad across the bridge of her nose. Big dark eyes, virtually pupil-less, the whites of them startling in their clarity. She went shoeless, but her feet were clean. The nails to her toes were pale and silver as fish scales.

—Mrs. Swanger is right. I do need help, Ada said, but what I need is in the way of rough work. Plowing, planting, harvesting, woodcutting, and the like. This place has to be made self-sufficient. I believe I need a man-hand for the job.

—Number one, the girl said, if you've got a horse I can plow all day. Number two, Old Lady Swanger told me your straits. Something for you to keep in mind would be that every man worth hiring is off and gone. It's a harsh truth, but that's mostly the way of things, even under favorable conditions.

The girl's name, Ada soon discovered, was Ruby, and though the look of her was not confidence-inspiring, she convincingly depicted herself as capable of any and all farm tasks. Just as importantly, as they talked, Ada found she was enormously cheered by Ruby. Ada's deep

impression was that she had a willing heart. And though Ruby had not spent a day of her life in school and could not read a word nor write even her name, Ada thought she saw in her a spark as bright and hard as one struck with steel and flint. And there was this: like Ada, Ruby was a motherless child from the day she was born. They had that to understand each other by, though otherwise they could not have been more alien to each other. In short order, and somewhat to Ada's surprise, they began striking a deal.

—CHARLES FRAZIER, FROM THE NOVEL

to work and not seeing all the Starbucks and Burger Kings. As a group, we were removed from everyday life and could concentrate solely on work."

Another remarkable turn of events on the Swanger Farm and Black Cove Farm locations was that both functioned as actual working farms. In the early spring of the previous year, the production's greens man, Roger Holden, had his crew plow and plant the fields. By the time the unit was filming on each of these tracts of land, the fields were yielding crops—corn, potatoes, beans, tomatoes, and various fruits. One of the unit's caterers availed himself of the vegetables and used them to feed the cast and crew.

There was, however, one drawback to filming in Romania during the summer of 2002: the weather. It rained for twenty-one days during the month of August, part of the precipitation that was drenching all of Europe at the time. Minghella, the cast and crew coped as best they could—switching locations at the last minute when possible, moving indoors or out, depending on the amount of rainfall, and sometimes waiting patiently for the rain to stop. In the end, and in spite of the weather, Minghella managed to stay on schedule and complete the summer sequences.

Then filming was temporarily suspended in Romania so that the unit could return to the United States for several weeks of work in South Carolina and Virginia. Production shut down over the Labor Day weekend of 2002 as the cast and crew packed their belongings and their equipment.

Cold Mountain was coming home to America.

ABOVE: Ray Winstone (Teague) and Charlie Hunnam (Bosie) on location. RIGHT: Renée Zellweger on ladder for the scene where Ruby inspects the roof at Black Cove Farm.

working with apples

Ada and Ruby spent much of the autumn working with apples. Apples had come in heavy and had to be picked, peeled, sliced and juiced: pleasant clean work, out among the trees handling the fruit. The sky for much of the time was cloudless blue, the air dry. The light, even at midday, brittle and raking, so that by angle alone it told of the year's waning. In the mornings they went carrying ladders when the dew still stood in the orchard grass. They'd climb among the tree limbs to fill sacks with apples, the ladders swaying as the limbs they were propped against gave under their weight. When all the sacks were full, they would bring the horse and sled to the orchard, haul them in, empty them and begin again.

–CHARLES FRAZIER, FROM HIS NOVEL

INT. ADA'S BEDROOM, BLACK COVE FARM. NIGHT. WINTER 1864

Ada in the bed, reading to Ruby from *Wuthering Heights*.

> **ADA**
> *My love for Linton is like the foliage in the woods. Time will change it like winter changes the trees. My love for Heathcliff resembles the eternal rocks beneath— a source of little visible delight. But necessary.*

> **RUBY**
> She ain't gonna marry Linton, is she? She said—*whatever our souls are made of, his and mine are the same.* You can't say that about Heathcliff and then marry Linton.

> **ADA**
> We'll find out. (*sleepy*) Tomorrow.

> **RUBY**
> I'm not waiting until tomorrow.

> **ADA**
> Ruby, I'm falling asleep.

She lies back in bed. Ruby takes the book, lies across the bottom of the bed, as Ada goes to sleep.

> **RUBY**
> *Little visible delight, but necessary.* I like that. . .

110

a vow to bear

Back in the U.S.A.

Production resumed on September 4, 2002, on the grounds of Botany Bay Plantation, a swampy expanse of wetland an hour outside of Charleston, South Carolina. Despite the success of shooting in Romania, it was clear to everyone that some of the locations in the Charleston area were crucial to the film.

Sydney Pollack says, "The kind of terrain that we were using in the south, low-lying swamp with large oak trees dripping Spanish moss, is essential to the way Anthony wanted to shoot the story. He portrays Inman's journey as a trek that begins at the seaside, moves through the swamps into the countryside, and crosses rolling hills on his way to Cold Mountain. Swampy terrain doesn't exist in Romania so by coming to South Carolina we captured it all."

In the end, about 20 percent of the movie was shot in the South, a far cry from the original intention of shooting entirely in the original region and even less than was anticipated when the decision to shoot in Romania was finalized. "We went to Romania thinking we would shoot half the film there and half the film here," explains Bill Horberg. "But it was apparent to us that it just made more and more sense to shoot as much as possible over there."

Still, while they were in the United States, the unit made the most of their time. In South Carolina, Minghella filmed the first of several scenes depicting the start of Inman's journey home with shoots of him trudging through a dead corn field, begging runaway slaves for an egg, and hiding from the Militia who come charging by on horseback looking for deserters.

Included in these scenes was the introduction of the Reverend Veasey (Philip Seymour Hoffman), a disgraced cleric. "My character, Reverend Veasey, is pretty tough to describe," admits Hoffman. "He's a mass of contradictions, like everyone else in the story, like everyone in life. He's a poor Reverend, not very good at his job. He's a man who believes in God and doing the right thing yet he is a philanderer. When Inman first sees him, Veasey is trying to get rid of a young slave woman who's pregnant with his child.

"Veasey is perfectly imperfect as a human being. From one moment to the next, he contradicts himself. In a way, the Reverend is kind of comic relief. I had to really let go of all the preconceived ideas I had about him and come to the part with an open heart."

Inman and Veasey travel together for a time, encountering the Ferry Girl (Jena Malone) who transports them on the run across the Cape Fear River and pays for it with her life. These episodes were also shot in Botany Bay.

Scenes of the wounded Inman getting his haircut were

LEFT: Shooting in Carter's Grove, Virginia, on the grounds of an antebellum mansion. RIGHT: Production crew wades knee-deep in the swamps of Botany Bay, South Carolina, to capture a shot of Jude Law (Inman) trekking through the water.

a world invisible to us

Inman did not consider himself to be a super-stitious person, but he did believe that there is a world invisible to us. He no longer thought of that world as heaven, nor did he still think that we get to go there when we die. Those teachings had been burned away. But he could not abide by a universe composed only of what he could see, especially when it was so frequently foul. So he held to the idea of another world, a better place, and he figured he might as well consider Cold Mountain to be the location of it as any-where.

–CHARLES FRAZIER, FROM HIS NOVEL

filmed in Charleston on the grounds of the College of Charleston, whose architecture dates back prior to the Civil War.

Two important scenes—one in which Inman, Veasey, and the chain gang prisoners to whom they are shackled, are paraded through town, and another in which Inman ties Veasey to a tree in front of a chapel in town and abandons him—were filmed in the center of Charleston's historic residential district in the area of Church and Queen Streets.

"We felt we couldn't have filmed this in any other place but Charleston," Ferretti says. "The architecture here, even as it exists today, is true to the period. Hardly any changes have occurred in the buildings and they've been perfectly maintained. It was mainly a matter of covering evidence of the modern day appurtenances." So streets were covered with dirt, real boardwalks replaced concrete, signage was redressed and weeds were planted. Suddenly it was 1864 in Charleston.

Then in the middle of production, news arrived that Jude Law's wife was about to give birth to their third child and work on the film was temporarily suspended for everyone. Law flew to London to be with his family and everyone took a very short break. A few days later, mother and baby doing well, Jude was back in Charleston and filming resumed.

Upon his return, Law filmed the scenes of a wounded Inman lying in a hospital bed barely able to speak as he recovers from his neck wound. These shots were filmed in a Charleston warehouse that Ferretti transformed into a soundstage. The sequence in which Inman and a group of wounded soldiers wade ankle deep in the river as part of their physical therapy was filmed at Botany Bay. The reverse shot, however, Inman and the patients returning to their beds, was shot hundreds of miles away in Carter's Grove, Virginia, on the grounds of an antebellum mansion that belongs to the historic area known as Colonial Williamsburg.

From here the unit moved to Richmond, Virginia. On September 17, 2002, they began shooting on the James River (which runs through the city) on a piece of wooded land called Belle Isle in the James River Park. Here they completed the sequence of Inman and Veasey traveling along the Cape Fear River on their way to their fateful encounter with the backwoodsman Junior (Giovanni Ribisi).

After nearly three weeks of filming in the South and a good deal of moving about, the unit packed up and returned to Romania. There were still three more months of work waiting for them in Eastern Europe.

footsteps in the snow

A Final Tour of Romania

The unit arrived back in Romania and resumed shooting on September 23, 2002. They began by shooting scenes on Black Cove Farm where Ruby Thewes first appears on Ada's porch and then continued to shoot scenes that chart their relationship, a crucial part of the storyline.

Following these sequences, Minghella returned to Inman's story to shoot the scene with Inman and Veasey when they encounter Junior (Giovanni Ribisi), a backwoodsman grappling with the body of a dead bull. Inman helps Junior and, in an apparent show of gratitude, Junior takes the men to his cabin, introduces his wife and her so-called sisters, gets them both stoned on bootleg liquor, and finally turns them over to the authorities. Inman and Veasey are put on a chain gang.

Giovanni Ribisi sees Junior in terms of his relation to Inman. "Junior is a completely decadent character," says Ribisi. "Willing to break every taboo, he lives a bacchanalian existence but is always on the look out for what's good for him. I see him as a character right out of *The Odyssey*, someone with his available women and his booze, who's there to be an obstacle for the hero."

In the story, Junior's cabin is located on swampland near the Cape Fear River. Ferretti constructed Junior's spread on one of Romania's few nature preserves near a town called Rece, an hour outside of the city of Brasov. For the sake of authenticity, he imported twenty enormous boxes of Spanish moss from South Carolina in order to dress the trees near the cabin to match what was filmed in the United States.

Following the scene at Junior's cabin, the unit moved to the town of Sinaia, an hour south of Brasov, where Minghella shot the awful conclusion to the Veasey episode against the rolling hills of the countryside there. Inman and Veasey, shackled to the chain gang, are led by Confederate guards in a kind of death march through the muddy, rugged countryside. When a group of Federals approach, the guardsmen open fire on the prisoners; Veasey is killed but Inman, though wounded, miraculously survives.

Inman is rescued at the conclusion of the sequence by Maddy (Eileen Atkins), a hermit who lives in a covered wagon hidden in the deepest reaches of the forest, surrounded by goats she uses as a means of survival: their coat for clothes, their milk and meat (after slaughtering a kid before Inman's eyes) for sustenance. Maddy nurses Inman back to health with her herbs and potions. She offers him some words of wisdom that he will later repeat to Ada. In Frazier's book Maddy tells him, "Our minds aren't made to hold on the particulars of pain the way we do bliss. It's a gift God gives us, a sign of His care for us."

LEFT: Giovanni Ribisi (Junior) at the start of his encounter with Jude Law (Inman) and Philip Seymour Hoffman (Veasey). RIGHT: The women of Junior's farm and Minghella taking a break from shooting.

Ultimately this is a film about people, in desperate
situations, who are searching for a reason to live.
And the reason they discover is love. So this is a
love story but on a grand scale. It takes place in
the heart of a time of great hardship and spiritual
turmoil. In the end, I came to understand that it's
a story about life, about finding a reason to live,
and about how love is the ultimate goal.

–Jude Law

Inman's next encounter is with Sara (Natalie Portman), a beautiful young war widow who lives with her sickly infant in a wooden cabin trying to survive. Inman takes shelter with the desperate woman; they comfort each other, only to be set upon by marauding Federals.

After these scenes were completed, Minghella began to shoot the final sequence of the film in which Inman finally returned to Cold Mountain.

The intimate and erotic scenes between Inman and Ada were filmed on a section of the abandoned Cherokee Village that Ferretti created in a converted warehouse soundstage in the city of Brasov. Then Minghella shot scenes in which a murderous Teague and his men confront Stobrod and companions on the killing ground, accusing them of being deserters.

Inman's return to Ada coincides with Teague intensifying the pursuit of his various prey, Ada among them. The Home Guard head, more murderous than ever as the war rages on, is closing in on Ada and Ruby, and in his quest discovers Stobrod (Brendan Gleeson), Pangle (Ethan Suplee), and Georgia (Jack White), another itinerant musician, camping out in what becomes known as the killing fields.

Ray Winstone who plays Teague, the murderous head of the Home Guard whose self-appointed mission is to execute Army deserters and local pacifists, worked with Minghella to ensure that the vicious character didn't devolve into a stereotype.

"As a character in the film Teague has become increasingly important," says Minghella. "His actions are so bleak that it's possible for the audience to see him simply as a two-dimensional villain." Minghella hired Ray Winstone for the part of Teague because he knew the talented actor was able to take the audience into the world of someone who behaves so badly. "Ray was capable of making the audience understand that the character's actions are based on longing and frustration, a sense of deprivation and self-loathing."

Winstone was up for the challenge and dug deep to discover motivations for his character. "Although Teague is a guy who goes around randomly killing deserters and people who live in his town, he acts within the context of what was going on in America at the time," Winstone explains.

"The guy has suffered a big loss, comparable to the kind of loss many Americans suffered during the Civil War. His land is occupied by someone else and he feels aggrieved about it. When the war breaks out, he sees a chance to reclaim his property and his position, to get back

a common mistake

To Inman's surprise, he found himself telling about Ada. He described her character and her person item by item and said the verdict he had come to at the hospital was that he loved her and wished to marry her, though he realized marriage implied some faith in a theoretical future, a projection of paired lines running forward through time, drawing nearer and nearer to one another until they became one line. It was a doctrine he could not entirely credit. Nor was he at all sure Ada would find his offer welcome, not from a man galled in body and mind as he had become. He concluded by saying though Ada was somewhat thistleish in comportment, she was, by his way of thinking, very beautiful. Her eyes were down-turned and set slightly asymmetrically in her head, and it gave her always a sad expression which in his view only served to point up her beauty.

The woman looked as if she thought Inman spoke the greatest foolishness she had ever heard. She pointed her pipe stem at him and said, You listen. Marrying a woman for her beauty makes no more sense than eating a bird for its singing. But it's a common mistake nonetheless.

—CHARLES FRAZIER, FROM HIS NOVEL

some of his own. It may not explain everything but it was a starting off point for me to understand the character."

Teague is also crucial to the final scenes of the movie—the reunion of Inman and Ada along with their disastrous encounter with Teague and his Home Guard in the killing fields. These scenes required a great deal of snow. It was Minghella's vision that, after Inman's trek through rain and swamp, through heat and killing humidity, across fields of corn and forests dense with trees, his reunion with Ada would take place in a vista of pure white snow.

Unfortunately, in a quirk of fate that can always occur with the weather, snowfall was light in Romania in the late fall of 2002. Although there was some snow in the area, in the end the filmmakers had to enhance what was on the ground with a quantity of fake snow created by special effects, an irony that was not wasted on the filmmakers. After all, they had come to Romania partly for the snow. (Ironically, back in the United States, the winter of 2002 produced record-breaking snowfalls throughout the country.)

"All you can do as a director is to play the percentage game," Minghella concedes, "which is to film in the place you believe you are most likely to get what you need to make the picture."

If, in the end, there wasn't as much snowfall in Romania as the filmmakers had hoped for, still, the benefits of shooting there more than compensated for the unpredictable weather. "The *Cold Mountain* shoot in Romania was an unqualified success," claims executive producer Iain Smith. "Other than a few minor glitches at the outset with the catering, we had no major problems. The film was delivered on time and on budget which is extraordinary when you consider we had to build the production process from the ground up in Eastern Europe."

Author Charles Frazier visited the unit in Charleston and Romania and expressed great satisfaction with the work of the cast and crew. "It was so interesting to see things that have been in your mind for so many years become very real and concrete. To see the characters embodied by these extraordinary actors, to see the intricate constructions that Dante created and to watch Anthony bring the world to life was beyond anything I hoped for. I knew I made a wise choice having these artists film my book, and it's certainly worked out that way."

After twenty-two weeks of shooting, production on *Cold Mountain* wrapped on December 14, 2002. The cast and crew returned home to their families and their lives. Many soon went on to other projects. But, for Anthony Minghella, work was hardly completed. Ahead of him was another twelve months of post-production.

SARA
I'm alone here, as you can see,
with my baby. I need to believe
you mean no harm.

*Inman takes out Maddy's flint-
lock. She starts, terrified.*

INMAN
No, I mean to give it to you.

*He turns its handle forwards and
offers it to her.*

SARA
I don't want it. I had my way
they'd take metal altogether
out of this world. Every blade,
every gun.

Hick's Farewell

My loving wife, my bosom friend
The object of my love
The time's been sweet I've spent with thee
My sweet, my harmless dove

How often you have looked for me
And oft times seen me come
But I must now depart from thee
And never more return

Though I must now depart from thee
Let this not grieve your heart
For you will shortly come to me
Where we shall never part

Lyrics from a song written during the Civil War
about a Confederate soldier trying to return home.
Charles Frazier listened to "Hick's Farewell" while
writing Cold Mountain *and Anthony Minghella*
listened to it while he was writing the screenplay.

the far side of trouble

PART THREE

Post-Production

bride bed full of blood

The Music of Cold Mountain

Throughout his novel, Charles Frazier refers to the saving grace of music. His characters play the piano, the banjo and the fiddle; they sing enthusiastically in church and at work; they sing in groups, they sing to each other, and they sing alone. Their songs express joy, sorrow, hope and despair. Music is everywhere in *Cold Mountain* and has the power to transform lives. Of Ruby's father, Stobrod, Frazier writes: "One thing he discovered with a great deal of astonishment was that music held more for him than just pleasure. There was meat to it. The grouping of sounds, their forms in the air as they rang out and faded, said something comforting to him about the role of creation. What the music said was that there is a right way for things to be ordered so that life might not always be just tangle and drift but have a shape, an aim. It was a powerful argument against the notion that things just happen."

In this passage, Frazier may as well have been describing the kind of emphasis Anthony Minghella, Gabriel Yared, Walter Murch, and T Bone Burnett put to incorporating music into *Cold Mountain*. Music is not only an essential element for these filmmakers, it is indispensable in telling a story, creating character, setting a mood and demonstrating that, as Frazier says, "there is a right way for things to be ordered."

To create a score for *Cold Mountain* Anthony Minghella turns to his longtime collaborator, composer Gabriel Yared. Minghella's relationship with Yared is complicated and demanding, in the best sense of those words. "With Gabriel, we've come up with this process where I never use anyone else's music but his," says Minghella, "which means he has to start writing the music during pre-production or when I'm filming. In this movie he wrote music for several of the pieces Ada plays on the piano. He wrote them while I was writing the screenplay so that the music grew with the film. I feel that that's a really organic way of working because the whole film is being nurtured at the same time."

Yared previously worked on *The English Patient* and *The Talented Mr. Ripley*. "On both occasions, he did a miraculously good job," Minghella says. "On a personal level, I care for him deeply—Gabriel is a real artist with an artist's vulnerability. Our working relationship is extremely personal and intimate. I'm in the room, often by his side, or reading the manuscript while he's composing. He is extremely modest about his music but meticulous and ferocious about how it should be performed."

Yared is completely devoted to Minghella and also sees their relationship as an extraordinary one. "We are like a young couple, each time reinventing a new vocabulary, reconsidering our relationship; each time is a new discovery for both of us. What are we going to discover today?" Yared says.

Yared began scoring *Cold Mountain* in April of 2002, several months before production

Wayfaring Stranger

I am a poor wayfaring stranger
Traveling through this world below
There is no sickness toil or danger
In that fair land to which I go

I'm going home to see my mother
I'm going home no more to roam
I am just going over to Jordan
I am just going over home

I know dark clouds will hover over me
I know my pathway's rough and steep
But golden fields lie out before me
Where weary eyes no more will weep

I'm going home to see my mother
I'm going home no more to roam
I am just going over to Jordan
I am just going over home

I'll soon be free from every trial
This form shall rest beneath the sword
I'll drop the cross of self denial
And enter in that home with God

*"Wayfaring Stranger" is the song that
Georgia (Jack White) sings to Ruby
(Renée Zellweger) toward the end of the
movie, during their Christmas party.*

began. This is unique in the business of making movies. Some composers start working during production, but most others wait until the movie is in a rough first cut.

Another departure from the norm is Minghella's refusal to use any temporary music tracks for the film during the cutting and testing process. Movies are difficult to watch without music and most often directors and editors put in tracks of music (often from other movies) that they think will work in the scene. This temporary track (called temp track) is then replaced by the composer's score when the film is complete.

"The thing that we do that creates the most pressure for Gabriel is that we don't use temp scores," Minghella explains. "Directors will use bits from various films, and I think that explains why so many scores sound exactly the same—because directors ask the composer to replicate the ideas on the temp track.

"I don't do that because I think it is very difficult to scrape temp music off the film and very hard to rid yourself of the stain of it. But it does make it very difficult for Gabriel, I'm afraid. Since there is no music unless it's his, well, that puts a lot of pressure on him to finish early so that the film can be previewed with the score. He welcomes the process but it is a nightmare for him," Minghella says. "I'm his greatest fan—he feels that, too—and I think it gives him the confidence to really extend himself. I know this process is torturous but I really feel it is the right way to compose music for film."

Yared's lyrical score permeates crucial scenes in the film such as Ada's piano playing in the fields, Inman's arrival at Cold Mountain, the lovemaking scene, and even the action on the killing ground. His original compositions are augmented with indigenous material, traditional nineteenth-century hymns and songs popular in the mountains at the time of the war. Included in the final score is a Stephen Foster song, "Ah May the Red Rose Live Always," arranged by Yared and sung by Nicole Kidman. Two hymns are heard in the Cold Mountain Chapel sequences, one is a Sing-Out Baptist standard, "Tarry with Me O My Savior," recorded with Ralph Stanley leading the choir. The other hymn, "I'm Going Home," is from the Sacred Harp book, a new form of choir singing that included hand gestures called Shape Note Singing that became popular in Southern Baptist churches at the time.

The hauntingly upbeat music Stobrod and Pangle play on the fiddle and banjo in the train car after the Petersburg battle is also traditional, "Spike Driver Blues" and "Coo Coo Bird." The songs in the Christmas celebration at the Old Mill, "Christmas Time Will Soon Be Over" and "Wayfaring Stranger," especially, may be recognizable to the audience. Minghella also uses a choir version of a hymn from the Scared Harp book, "Am I Born to Die," over sections of the battle scene and when Stobrod plays for the dying Oakley. A traditional song as remembered by Ralph Stanley, "Great High Mountain," is heard at the end of the film. All of

RIGHT: Tintype image created by photographer Stephen Berkman of Ethan Suplee (Pangle), Jack White (Georgia), and Brendan Gleeson (Stobrod).

this music was recorded during pre-production and produced by T Bone Burnett, an expert in the field.

Burnett, who produced the music for *O Brother, Where Art Thou?*, describes the indigenous songs used in *Cold Mountain* as "some of the very earliest rock and roll music." Dating as far back as the 1400s, the songs have their roots in Scotland, England, Ireland, and Africa. "Black people and white people were not in church together, but they were in the trenches together," Burnett adds. "These songs, which came from the church and the whorehouse, have been recorded in hundreds of different forms. They and their antecedents make up a large part of what we think of as American popular music. They are what Nick Tosches calls 'the twisted roots of rock and roll.' We wanted Jack White to play Georgia because he is a great rock-and-roll singer."

Burnett notes that Frazier's book is replete with references to songs like "Wayfaring Stranger." "Many of the songs in the movie were mentioned in the book," Burnett points out. "Frazier is obviously very interested in Southern heritage music, and it was important to us that he be happy with the way this stuff came out. These songs are important to who we are in this country. The music grew out of the black mud like vines around a tree, but it has spread all over the world."

The indigenous songs were recorded as naturalistically as possible. "We used minimum technology," Burnett says, "and we restricted ourselves to instruments they would have had back there in those days, and we used old ones of those."

Many of the actors in the movie were also musicians, "We were very lucky with the cast in terms of music," says Anthony Minghella. "Brendan Gleeson plays Stobrod, a fiddle player, and he actually plays the fiddle."

The character of Georgia in the film is practically a singing role, and Minghella cast Jack White of White Stripes for the part. "I didn't expect to feature his acting," Minghella confesses, "but Jack was so good on screen that I went back and wrote lines for him. And then, of course, Nicole is a real pianist. She plays and sings beautifully and that adds a bit of magic to her characterization of Ada."

Mention must also be made of Dirk Powell, who played the banjo when the music was recorded and was the on-set music advisor. Other musicians who recorded the music for the film include Norman Blake, Ralph Stanley, Stuart Duncan, Tim O'Brien, Tim Eriksen, Riley Baugus, and Mike Compton.

My character, Stobrod, is a ne'er-do-well, a drinker and a
traveling musician. In the beginning of the movie, he is asked
to play for a dying boy and that experience transforms his
relationship with music. It is like he finds a door to uncover
his soul. After that scene, he disappears for awhile only to
reemerge later in the film as another kind of person. He
wants to reconcile with his daughter and to get her to see
him as a different kind of man. There are many journeys in
Cold Mountain and, in the end, they all converge. Stobrod's
journey begins and ends with the music; for him, the music
leads him to enlightenment and, hopefully, to salvation.

–BRENDAN GLEESON

a satisfied mind

Editing

In London, editor and sound design artist Walter Murch shares a suite of offices with Anthony Minghella while Gabriel Yared composes nearby. Together the three men will spend almost a year of post-production, starting in January of 2003, to bring *Cold Mountain* to the screen. Film editors usually work in relative obscurity, at least in terms of the general public. Murch, however, has had such a legendary career that he is the exception to the rule.

Walter Murch mixed the sound on *American Graffiti* (1973) and *The Godfather Part II* (1974), won a double British Academy Award for sound mixing and film editing on *The Conversation* (1974), for which he was also nominated by the American Academy, won his first Oscar for mixing *Apocalypse Now* (1979), and won unprecedented double Oscars for sound mixing and film editing for his work on *The English Patient* (1996). "One of the things I find hilarious in my building in London is that when people come here, they ask, "Is it true that Walter Murch is upstairs?" notes Minghella. "He has emerged from relative invisibility into being an icon. His reputation extends beyond any particular film or award. If any of us will be remembered, it will be him."

Murch is so highly regarded as an innovator in his field, that when he tries something new, Hollywood pays attention. On December 4, 2002, the *Hollywood Reporter* featured a lead story on the editor's decision to use new technology on *Cold Mountain*. "Esteemed editor Walter Murch sent ripples of surprise through the editing community when he decided to use Final Cut Pro to cut Anthony Minghella's *Cold Mountain*, due out Christmas 2003, for Miramax. That decision has prompted some in the feature community to take a closer look at Apple's desktop-based system."

Walter Murch is always prepared to try something new. "I guess it is just part of my personality to get interested in a certain approach and take off in that direction without waiting for everything to be completely bolted down, trusting that somehow things will turn out all right as we go along. Actually, working with Final Cut is like playing on a different piano. If you had become accustomed to a certain manufacture of piano, and then suddenly switched to another, it would take a while to learn the touch of the new instrument. I had been using the Avid since *English Patient*, and the Final Cut 'piano' is an equivalent, but different instrument. As it turned out, I became comfortable with Final Cut very quickly."

ABOVE: Walter Murch working on an edit of Cold Mountain *at the Kodak Cinelabs in Bucharest, Romania. Photo by his son, Walter Slater Murch. LEFT: Production still of Ruby (Renée Zellweger) and Stobrod (Brendan Gleeson) who plays her father in the film.*

a satisfied mind

The array of computers and editing equipment that Murch took to Romania was the first large-scale motion picture digital editing system based on Final Cut Pro software. "There are many things I like about Final Cut, but the most appealing is that it is economical and portable without sacrificing quality—all you basically need is the program and the Apple computer. The software is so inexpensive compared to the Avid that there is practically no limit to the number of stations that could be opened with anyone's PowerBook, or even iBook."

Technology, however, can only take you so far. "Avid or Final Cut Pro can design certain things to make the editor's job easier," Murch points out. "But no matter what tool you are using, the creative task of editing the film requires a certain set of skills—above all a sense of story and rhythm."

Murch has edited picture and mixed sound for Minghella since *The English Patient* and

gets involved in the project early on, starting with the development of the screenplay. "This is our third film together and, as on the previous two, Anthony would send out early drafts of the screenplay to all the heads of departments," says Murch. "The first thing that struck me was that *Cold Mountain* had a different story structure from our past two films. *Ripley* was played in linear time, all from one person's point of view: Tom Ripley was in every scene. *English Patient* was the opposite, in that it had multiple combinations of characters and consequently multiple points of view as well as a nonlinear time structure with many transitions backwards and forwards in time and place. In a way, *Cold Mountain* is a hybrid of those two earlier films. Like *Ripley*, everything in Inman's story is told from his point of view. The same is true for Ada and her story. It is only towards the end of the film that there are scenes that don't involve either of them, for instance the sequence around the campfire with Stobrod and Teague.

"But like *English Patient*, the Inman/Ada stories are also shifting back and forth in time and place," Murch explains. "At the beginning of the film, we go back to learn how Inman met Ada, the girl in the tintype. So Inman's story is established as the film's 'present' and Ada's is in the past. It is not until after Ada's father dies that the two narratives start to become contemporaneous. For example, the scene where Inman meets Veasey takes place early one morning and, at exactly the same moment back in Cold Mountain, Ruby is waking up Ada. By this point in the film, Ada's story has had to 'catch up' to Inman's, which is tricky. How do we accomplish that shift?

ABOVE and LEFT: These images, called "screen grabs," are from Walter Murch's editing program for Cold Mountain. *These low-res scans identify specific scenes and enable the editor to move scenes around while constructing the film. The images form storyboards, as seen behind Walter Murch in the photo of him on the previous page. The image shown above, of a rabbit on the battlefield, is currently the opening shot of the movie.*

145

"Well, as it turns out," Murch continues, "it takes place in the section of the film where Inman has been hospitalized and receives a letter from Ada bringing him up to date on everything that has happened to her since he left Cold Mountain. During these scenes, Ada's time frame is warping to catch up to Inman's—to the 'present' of the film. The audience needs to recognize that this is going on but not become overly conscious of it. It should be interesting but not confusing. As it actually worked out, this is something that was not in the screenplay, but rather a development in the editing. We're still working on getting it exactly right, and every version of the film has been different in this regard. I've never confronted a problem like this one before. But that's exactly the kind of challenge that I love."

Problem solving is a major part of any editor's job and Murch handles that aspect with a calm assurance. Although some people expected that shooting and editing in Romania would be extremely challenging, Murch has nothing but praise for the working conditions in that country. "Romania allowed for a faithfulness to the time and place we were after. The Carpathian Mountains in Romania in 2002 were standing in for the Appalachian Mountains of the 1860s, and it struck me that the two places even shared the same phonetic ending. There is so little development in Romania that Anthony was able to photograph huge vistas in 360 degrees without worrying about any modern intrusions. The remoteness also meant that we never had a problem with twenty-first–century noises encroaching on the sound track. Sonically speaking, we were 140 years back in time."

While filming in Romania, Murch maintained an editorial office at the Kodak Cinelabs in Bucharest that had been constructed in 1999. "It was the first time in my experience that I had done my editing in a film laboratory. I was a little apprehensive, but it turned out to be very pleasant and efficient," notes Murch. "In the five months of shooting we processed just under 1 million feet of negative through the lab in Bucharest—everything went smoothly and the photographic quality was astonishing. Plus there was telecine, sound transfer, and 35mm projection all within twenty paces of my editing room. I wish I could lift up the whole place and take it around the world with me. The only truly difficult things about working in Romania, for us at least, were the customs procedures of getting equipment in and out of the country. It took

ABOVE: Walter Murch and Anthony Minghella in their Mirage office at the Old Chapel Studios in London where the film is being cut.

about a week to ship stuff from London. Romania is applying for membership in the European Union, and in a few years, many things will have changed procedurally and culturally to allow for a more easy exchange of equipment."

Like all of Minghella's "kitchen cabinet of collaborators" and for all the obvious reasons, Murch is held in very high esteem by the director. "He has a brain as big as a house," says Minghella, "he is well read, inquisitive, lugubrious, and volatile and he can range from the monosyllabic or the monologue—feast or famine—either talk nonstop or not say anything at all. My relationship with Walter is the most significant relationship for me in the making of the movie. He has taught me so much—it is a mix of education and intellectual fistfighting. And," adds Minghella, "he tells me off more than anyone else I work with."

The Fortune Cookies

Homemade fortune cookies are part of a long tradition between Walter Murch and Anthony Minghella.

Many years ago, Murch was reading the journals of the acclaimed French director Robert Bresson who, though he only made ten films in a thirty-year career, is revered as one of the most original and creative figures in cinema. Jean Cocteau once wrote that Bresson, "expresses himself cinematically as a poet would with his pen." Bresson's thoughts on filmmaking were compiled in a book called *Notes on Cinematography* and published in English in 1977. Murch is a great fan of the book. "Bresson wrote in an epigrammatic style and many of the things he wrote struck me as true about the business of making films," says Murch. "I thought they read like fortune cookies."

For Christmas presents one year, Murch found a place in San Francisco where you could have your own fortunes placed in cookies. He had cookies made with Bresson's epigrams.

All together Murch has compiled about 120 of these epigrams, adding a few other voices (such as Cocteau and Rilke) to the collection. *Cold Mountain*'s shoot was scheduled for 113 days, so Murch put all his epigrams into a prescription bottle and presented them to Minghella at the beginning of production. "I told him, 'Take one a day but don't operate any heavy machinery,'" says Murch. "And frequently it seemed as though the fortune was talking about the specific problem he was facing that day."

The following is a brief sampling of Murch's cookie collection.

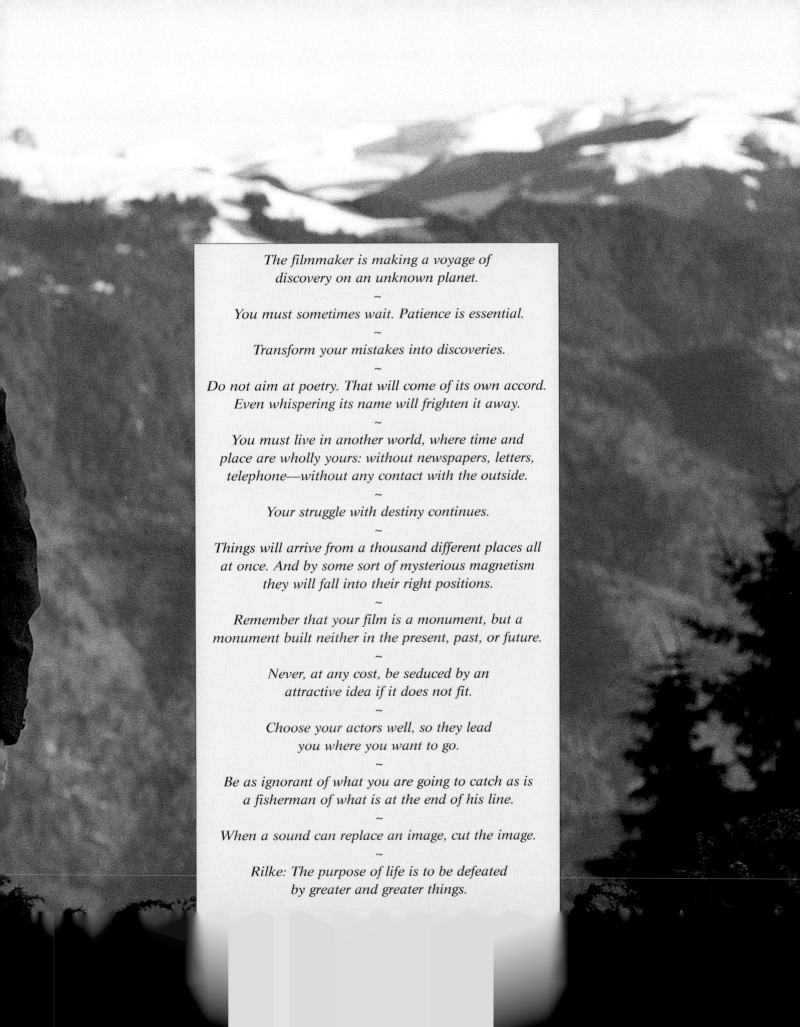

*The filmmaker is making a voyage of
discovery on an unknown planet.*

~

You must sometimes wait. Patience is essential.

~

Transform your mistakes into discoveries.

~

*Do not aim at poetry. That will come of its own accord.
Even whispering its name will frighten it away.*

~

*You must live in another world, where time and
place are wholly yours: without newspapers, letters,
telephone—without any contact with the outside.*

~

Your struggle with destiny continues.

~

*Things will arrive from a thousand different places all
at once. And by some sort of mysterious magnetism
they will fall into their right positions.*

~

*Remember that your film is a monument, but a
monument built neither in the present, past, or future.*

~

*Never, at any cost, be seduced by an
attractive idea if it does not fit.*

~

*Choose your actors well, so they lead
you where you want to go.*

~

*Be as ignorant of what you are going to catch as is
a fisherman of what is at the end of his line.*

~

When a sound can replace an image, cut the image.

~

*Rilke: The purpose of life is to be defeated
by greater and greater things.*

**EXT. ADA AND RUBY HUT, CHERO-
KEE VILLAGE. NIGHT. WINTER 1864**

Inman is outside his cabin. Only the lights
escaping from the cabin fire lights them,
almost silhouettes.

INMAN
I'm sorry. I was trying to be quiet.

ADA
I couldn't sleep.

INMAN
—I got no appetite left to be in a room
with wounded men.

ADA
I can't see your face.

INMAN
It's not a face you recognized.

ADA
Did you get my letters?

INMAN
I got three letters. Carried them in that
book you gave me. The Bartram.

ADA
I probably sent 103. Did you write
to me?

INMAN
Whenever I could. If you never got
them I can summarize.

ADA
No, it's —

INMAN
I pray you're well. I pray I'm in your
thoughts. You are all that keeps me
from sliding into some dark place.

ADA
But how did I keep you? We barely
knew each other. A few moments.

INMAN
A thousand moments. They're like a
bag of tiny diamonds. Don't matter if
they're real or things I made up. The
shape of your neck. The way you felt
under my hands when I pulled you
to me.

ADA
You're plowing a field.

INMAN
You're carrying a tray.

ADA
I'm playing the piano and you're
standing outside. You wouldn't come
in. That's why I had to carry a tray.

INMAN
That kiss — which I've kissed every
day of my walking.

ADA

Every day of my waiting.

INMAN

Maybe you can't see my face, but if you could see my inside, my whatever you want to name it, my spirit, that's the fear I have—I think I'm ruined. They kept trying to put me in the ground, but I wasn't ready, no ma'am. But if I had goodness, I lost it. If I had anything tender in me I shot it dead.

Ruby stomps out of the hut.

RUBY

Number one — shut this door, it's freezing.
(*goes over to Stobrod's hut*)
Number two—shut that door, it's freezing.
(*turns to them*)
I'm laying on my back, with my fingers poked in my ears trying to shut out who's got a bag of diamonds and who's carrying a tray. If you want to get three feet up a bull's ass listen to what sweethearts whisper to each other.

When she reached the place, the boy had already gathered up the horses and gone. She went to the men on the ground and looked at them, and then she found Inman apart from them. She sat and held him in her lap. He tried to talk, but she hushed him. He drifted in and out and dreamed a bright dream of a home. It had a cold-water spring rising out of rock, black dirt fields, old trees. In his dream the year seemed to be happening all at one time, all the seasons blending together. Apple trees hanging heavy with fruit but yet unaccountably blossoming, ice rimming the spring, okra plants blooming yellow and maroon, maple leaves red as October, corn tops tasseling, a stuffed chair pulled up to the glowing parlor hearth, pumpkins shining in the fields, laurels blooming on the hillsides, ditch banks full of orange jewelweed, white blossoms on dogwood, purple on redbud. Everything coming around at once. And there were white oaks, and a great number of crows, or at least the spirits of crows, dancing and singing in the upper limbs. There was something he wanted to say.

An observer situated up on the brow of the ridge would have looked down on a still, distant tableau in the winter woods. A creek, remnants of snow. A wooded glade, secluded from the generality of mankind. A pair of lovers. The man reclined with his head in the woman's lap. She, looking down into his eyes, smoothing back the hair from his brow. He, reaching an arm awkwardly around to hold her at the soft part of her hip. Both touching each other with great intimacy. A scene of such quiet and peace that the observer on the ridge could avouch to it later in such a way as might lead those of glad temperaments to imagine some conceivable history where long decades of happy union stretched before the two on the ground.

—CHARLES FRAZIER, FROM THE NOVEL

black bark in winter,
white blossoms in spring

The Screenings

The first cut of *Cold Mountain*, completed in the summer of 2003 ran for three hours and was ready to be put through the test-by-fire all films must endure: test screenings. "Test screenings are a blessing and a curse. But I am the wrong person to ask," admits Sydney Pollack. "I think you have to be like a doctor; not listen to the patient. I get hell from everybody, particularly Harvey [Weinstein] for not testing my own pictures. I don't do it because then I am making their movie, not my movie. But, will I test my next movie? Yes, I've adjusted to the fact that I have to test them."

Audiences for Miramax screenings are not chosen at random though they ultimately do comprise a random sampling of people. Tentative participants are interviewed to determine several factors such as their film tastes, economic status, age, and other criteria. The purpose is to engage a diversified but mainstream group of people who can articulate their reactions to the filmmakers. "We don't want to load the audience with people who only like action/adventure or science fiction movies," explains Ron Yerxa.

Every production company has their own method for test screenings as well as their favorite locations. Miramax Films likes to screen their movies in Edgewater, New Jersey, a suburban community about forty-five minutes outside of Manhattan. There, the company has always been able to recruit a wide range of people.

Consequently, the first screening for *Cold Mountain* was held in Edgewater on July 21, 2003. "Anything can happen the first time you show your movie," says Yerxa, "especially when you are presenting a three-hour film to an audience who does not know what to expect."

After the test screening, twenty-two people from the audience are selected to participate in a focus group. Supervised by a neutral moderator, the group is presented with a series of questions that measure their reaction to the film. What did they like? What didn't they like? What would they change? Was the length of the film a problem? And, most importantly: Would they recommend the movie to their friends?

The results of *Cold Mountain*'s first screening were encouraging to everyone. "The headline was: It played extremely well," says Yerxa.

A month later, a second screening was held, again in Edgewater, New Jersey, and with an audience that was demographically similar to the first one. Minor changes had been made to the film and seven minutes had been cut from screen time.

Again the movie tested extremely well.

A third screening was scheduled for Los Angeles but then the filmmakers decided they should go south and test the film in the area where it takes place. They wanted to know how

Southerners would react to *Cold Mountain*. Would they have different responses than their northern counterparts?

Almost any city in the South would have suited their purposes but they settled on Charleston, South Carolina, because Anthony Minghella was scheduled to be in Charleston in late August to shoot some helicopter scenes. So, *Cold Mountain*'s third screening took place on August 27, 2003, and proved a point that delighted the filmmakers: The film played just as well in the south as it had in the north.

As this book goes to press, in the late summer of 2003, *Cold Mountain* is still in the final stages of being edited. The filmmakers continue to tweak certain scenes. They try to resolve issues of sequencing and deal with the dilemma of the opening credits. Do the titles at the beginning of the movie distract from the start of the storyline? Some say they do. So the team is considering the idea of opening the movie without credits and running the titles at the end of the film. They discuss which scenes might be cut or at least shortened. They wonder: Will the three-hour running time be a problem for the audience?

The possibilities for last-minute alterations are endless and can turn fine-tuning a movie into a grueling task. Eventually, the filmmakers will run out of time. A final cut must be delivered for the film's Christmas 2003 release.

Right now, as fall approaches, almost three years after Minghella first sat down to write his screenplay, everyone involved in the movie expresses a great deal of satisfaction and contentment with the film. Feelings are very, very positive and expectations are high.

"My hope is that *Cold Mountain* will prove that there is a market and an audience for classic filmmaking," says Sydney Pollack. "That is, movies not necessarily dependent on special effects; movies that can crossover age groups and appeal to middle-aged and older people and still reach young people. Movies have to reach young people and, in an historical film, everyone's fear is that it won't. My big hope is that *Cold Mountain* will validate the conviction that if you make a classic movie, it will reach a wide audience."

Whether that will happen or not is anyone's guess. In Hollywood, no one ever knows how the general public will react to any given movie. It is simply the nature of the business. Great movies don't sell tickets; bad movies become box office blockbusters. Unexpected political and economic events can make or break a film. Almost anything can happen. Each time out is a gamble and test screenings can only go so far as a barometer of how the ever-fickle public will react.

To predict the success of *Cold Mountain*, the filmmakers might as well break open one of Walter Murch's fortune cookies. Perhaps this one: *You will not know 'til much later if your film is worth the mountain range of efforts it is costing you.*

if you go on

What you have lost will not be returned to you. It will always be lost. You're left with only your scars to mark the void. All you can choose to do is go on or not. But if you go on, it's knowing you carry your scars with you.

—CHARLES FRAZIER, FROM HIS NOVEL

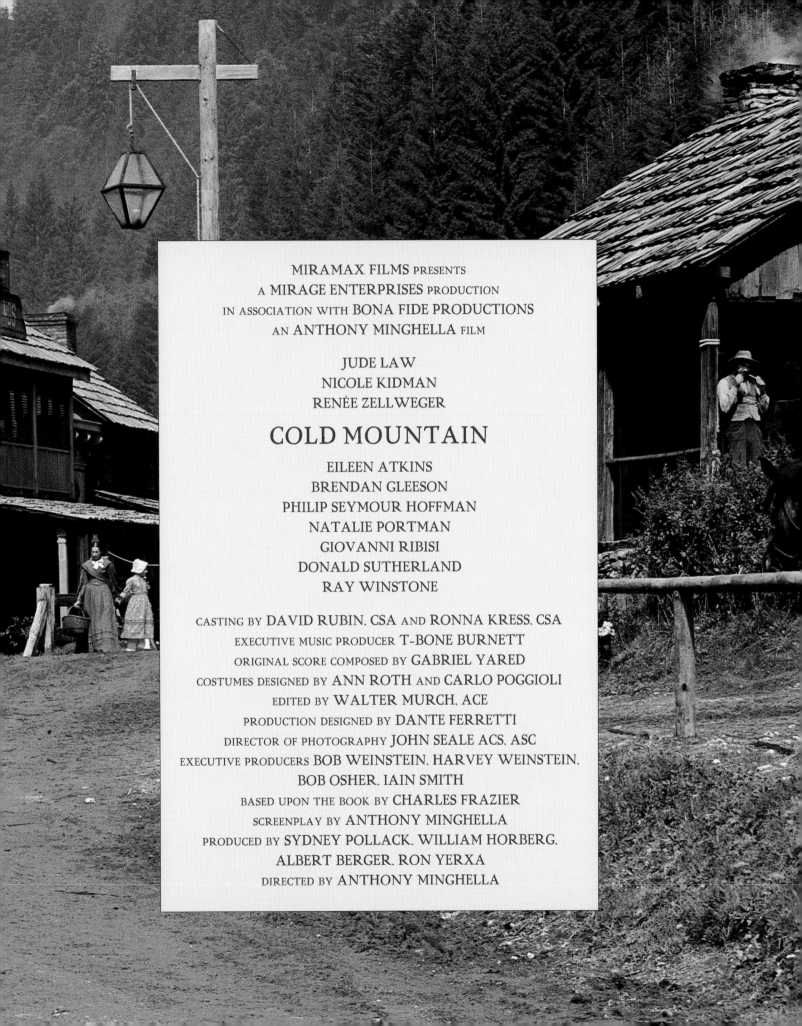

behind-the-scenes photographs

by Brigitte Lacombe

ABOUT THE AUTHOR AND DIRECTOR/SCREENWRITER OF COLD MOUNTAIN

CHARLES FRAZIER grew up in the mountains of North Carolina. He now lives in Raleigh with his wife and daughter, where they raise horses. *Cold Mountain* is his first novel.

ANTHONY MINGHELLA's first film as a writer/director—*Truly, Madly, Deeply*—was a great success both in Britain and in the U.S., winning several awards. *The English Patient*, which he adapted for the screen and directed, has won more than 30 awards, including nine 1996 Academy Awards, including Best Picture and Best Director, two Golden Globe awards, and six BAFTAs. *The Talented Mr. Ripley*, which Minghella adapted for the screen and directed, was nominated for five 1999 Academy Awards, including Best Adapted Screenplay, and for seven BAFTAs, including Best Film, Best Director, and Best Adapted Screenplay. In 2003, Anthony Minghella was named the head of the British Film Institute.

PHOTOGRAPH CREDITS

All photographs by Phil Bray, except those noted on the following pages: Stephen Berkman 17, 76, 137; Bill Horberg 33, 36, 58, 65 (top), 88; Brigitte Lacombe 161-191; Michelle Pizanis 82-83; and Demmie Todd 1, 23, 24-25, 51 (bottom right), 100 (inset), 112, 113, 114-115, 116, 117 (top and bottom).

ACKNOWLEDGMENTS

We are indebted to many people for their special contributions to the creation of this beautiful book. Among them:

At Miramax Films: Jason Cassidy, Gary Faber, Ethan Noble, Holly Landon, Christine Edwards, Geraldine Agoncillo, Pamela Cruz, Tom Piechura, Jonathan Seliger, and Devereux Chatillon.

At Bona Fide Productions: Producers Albert Berger and Ron Yerxa. At Mirage Enterprises: Producers Sydney Pollack and Bill Horberg, as well as Cassius Matthias, Ralph Millero, and Donna Ostroff, and, especially, Tim Bricknell, who also served as Associate Producer on the film.

All members of the *Cold Mountain* production team, including Dante Ferretti, Ann Roth, Gabriel Yared, T Bone Burnett, Walter Murch, Walter Murch, Jr., Iain Smith, David Rubin, and Dianne Dreyer.

For providing so many wonderful images for our selection: Stephen Berkman, Michelle Pizanis, Demmie Todd, and, especially, Phil Bray. A special note of thanks to Brigitte Lacombe and Janet Johnson for enabling us to include the Lacombe special section.

For contributing his wonderful foreword and extracts from his novel: Charles Frazier, and thanks to Katherine Frazier and Atlantic Monthly Books for helping to make this possible.

For contributions to the text: Dan Auiler, Larry Kaplan, and especially to project editor Linda Sunshine. For the beautiful book design: Timothy Shaner of Night & Day Design, and his associate, Christopher Measom. For bringing it all together, the always professional and flexible Newmarket Press staff: Frank DeMaio, Keith Hollaman, Shannon Berning, Paul Sugarman, Heidi Sachner, Harry Burton, Tracey Bussell, Tara Hoffman, and Maina Lopotukhin.

And, of course, Anthony Minghella, whose vision, passion, and patience helped to make this book possible. Thank you all.

—Esther Margolis, publisher, Newmarket Press

Has Anyone Seen

For Phyllis Root and Amy Ehrlich,
with love and thanks
—N. F. M.

First edition 2007

Library of Congress Cataloging-in-Publication Data is available.

Library of Congress Catalog Card Number 2006051828

ISBN 978-0-7636-1384-6

2 4 6 8 10 9 7 5 3 1

Printed in China

This book was typeset in Colwell.
The illustrations were done in watercolor.

Candlewick Press
2067 Massachusetts Avenue
Cambridge, Massachusetts 02140

visit us at www.candlewick.com

My Emily Greene?

Norma Fox Mazer
illustrated by Christine Davenier

CANDLEWICK PRESS
CAMBRIDGE, MASSACHUSETTS

Has anyone seen my Emily Greene?

She's my barefoot dancer,
my brown-eyed prancer,
my girl who loves the color red,
and roses and rhymes and ribbons and bread.

Has anyone seen my Emily Greene?

Her lunch is ready. It's half past noon.
The table's set — knife, fork, and spoon.
I've made oodles of noodles, brown-sugar ham,
and fresh-baked bread with strawberry jam.

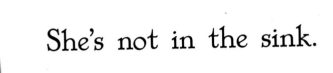
Has anyone seen my Emily Greene?

She's not in the sink.

She's not in the drawer.

She's not in the pantry

or behind the door.

Is she under the rug?

Behind the chair?

On top of the desk?

Way up in the air?

I can't find her anywhere.

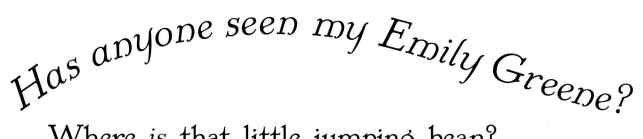

Has anyone seen my Emily Greene?

Where *is* that little jumping bean?
She must be hungry—it's time for lunch.
I want her, I need her, I miss her a bunch.

I'll look in the tub.

I'll comb through my hair.

I'll pull up the shade.

Oh, no! She's not there!

Should I peek in this corner?
Shake out these socks?

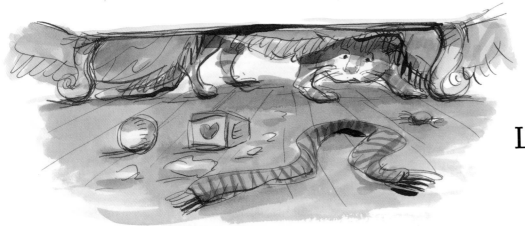

Look under the bed?

Open this box?

Wait! Wait! What's that I hear?

A knock . . .
knock . . .
knock . . .
at the door . . .

a stamp . . .
stamp . . .
stamp . . .
on the floor . . .

Who could it be?

I see! I see!
It's my Emily Greene,
right in front of me!
Here she is, before my eyes—

Emily Greene, what a surprise!

Come to the table. Sit on your chair.
Yes, my sweetie, that one there.

Put on your napkin. Pick up your spoon.
Here's your lunch. Don't leave too soon.

My little one, my honey bun.

My daisy fluff, my sweet big stuff.

My clever, my funny, my lovely, my sunny.

My daughter so dear.

My Emily Greene . . . right here.